PAPUA NEW GUINEA

Social Science

Grade 7

Teacher Resource Book

Stephen Ranck

OXFORD

Level 8, 737 Bourke Street, Docklands, Victoria 3008, Australia

Oxford University Press is a department of the University of Oxford. It furthers the University's objective of excellence in research, scholarship, and education by publishing worldwide in

Oxford New York

Auckland Cape Town Dar es Salaam Hong Kong Karachi
Kuala Lumpur Madrid Melbourne Mexico City Nairobi
New Delhi Shanghai Taipei Toronto

With offices in

Argentina Austria Brazil Chile Czech Republic France Greece
Guatemala Hungary Italy Japan Poland Portugal Singapore
South Korea Switzerland Thailand Turkey Ukraine Vietnam

First published 2007
Reprinted 2007, 2008, 2009, 2010, 2014, 2025

ISBN 978 0 19 555513 4

Typeset by Cathy Rose
Printed in China by Golden Cup Printing Co. Ltd

Oxford University Press Australia & New Zealand is committed to sourcing paper responsibly.

Contents

Overview

Social Science Grade 7

Social Science Grade 7 Student Book continues and expands on *Social Science Grade 6 Student Book*. Students should be able to use much of what they learned in Grade 6. For example, they can apply ideas such as roles, rights, and rituals to some of the new material in Grade 7. The Grade 7 book expands knowledge from the local situation to the province, the nation and the region. This allows students to explore many exciting new areas.

Papua New Guinea has interesting and varied neighbours to the north, east, south and west. One good way to learn about Papua New Guinea as a nation is to compare it in many different ways to its neighbours. This approach allows students to learn both about the region and the nation. Again building on the Grade 6 work, students can begin to compare national values and attitudes.

The governments, economies and cultures of Papua New Guinea and all the countries in the region are rapidly changing. This means that learning will require much more investigation. Students will need to seek out information to bring materials up to date.

A major resource will be radio and newspaper items about the nation and the region. Studies may go in many different directions as students compare what is happening in Papua New Guinea to what is happening in other countries of the region. The teacher will need to carefully guide class research to balance bias and prejudice that may be evident in news sources. Examples of news articles are provided here, with suggestions for student work, but you should also look for recent examples that will be relevant and of interest to your students.

As a teacher, you can challenge students to see how many ways they can find current information. There will be current events in the nation and region for each of the chapters in this text. Make it a game for students to find out what is happening now. This can be done as a game throughout the school year. Students must seek out and bring current information about the topics under study to class. You can have a reward for the best news or relevant ideas of the week. Sources of information will be the press and other printed materials. It should also involve people in the community to include student's families as well as other community members. This theme will be followed through the guide.

Using the Student Book

Key features

The *Grade 7 Social Science Student Book* consists of four chapters that closely follow the syllabus. Each chapter covers one strand and one sub-strand. Some of the sub-strands have been divided into sections to make it easier for the students and teacher to follow.

Overview: The syllabus is ambitious for Grade 7 students, as it covers very large areas of social science, including physical and environmental science. Teachers will have to judge the levels that Grade 7 students can achieve given the resources available. Getting current information is very important, as the societies, governments and economies of the provinces, the nation and the region are constantly changing. The text can provide a foundation, teaching about processes and the past. Teachers and students must find material to keep information updated to the present. Students can then consider what may happen in the future. In some urban areas, students will have access to the Internet, allowing them to research many topics. Other students may be limited to radio and newspapers for current information on social, political and economic development in their province, in the nation of Papua New Guinea and in the region.

This guide also provides more detailed information for some of the more complex areas of the syllabus like scales, latitude and longitude on maps. This can help where students have special interests or questions.

Chapter 1 looks at the people and environment of the region, including natural hazards. Papua New Guinea has some very interesting neighbours. It has an interesting physical geography and geology that explain much of the environment. Map reading skills are expanded from Grade 6 to look at the larger areas covered by Grade 7.

Chapter 2 covers government (or civic) studies, an overview to the history of government in the region and resource development in the region. It closes with a look at some resources in the region.

Chapter 3 explores culture and cultural expression through an examination of photographs. This should be an enjoyable way for students to start to grasp the richness of culture in the region. It should also help them see the different cultural influences that have spread across many parts of the region. It also provides a model that students can build on by collecting their own pictures. They may follow any theme they wish in cultural expressions. Grade 6 looked at many iconic cultural expressions such as painting, sculpture, song, dance and architecture. Grade 7 focuses on many of the more day-to-day national cultural expressions found in the region. Students can also revisit Grade 6 materials and how they apply to the expanded geographic coverage of Grade 7.

Chapter 4 challenges students to do project work that integrates the strands and sub-strands that they have studied in the first three chapters. The integrated project can begin at any time in the course. However, for most Grade 7 students, the end of the course will be the easiest time to complete this. Students will need your guidance as the teacher. The key is to maintain balance and consider all sides of an argument or problem. As the teacher, you can encourage your students to find an integrating project that they are really interested in doing. The more interest they have, the better they will do.

Using the Teacher Resource Book

This Teacher Resource Book provides a guide to teaching Social Science for Grade 7.

Key features

Students will be pursuing information about events in their province, the nation and the region. Much of this information will carry attitudes and values. There will be prejudice and bias in radio, newspaper and other current information. The teacher's task is to help students achieve balance. This can be done by comparing or discussing all the available information. Have the class examine the attitudes and values that they find in the different materials. As students study political, economic and government issues they will come across information that will need balance and discussion.

When students interview people to gain information, it is a good idea to be sure this is done in groups or with adult supervision. There may be times when it is appropriate for groups of males to interview males and female groups to interview females.

We continue to follow a simplified social science process: SEE – UNDERSTAND – ACT. The second step could also be called CONSIDER; EVALUATE; or APPRAISE. (The syllabus uses the term judge, but this could confuse students.)

The three-step process includes the following skills:

- SEE: form questions, prepare a study, gather information
- UNDERSTAND: analyse and evaluate the information, make conclusions (but understand that more information later may change your conclusions)
- ACT: present the information or take action (and then consider the results again)

How to use it

When you receive this book you need to:

- review it to get an idea of the information it contains and its organisation
- consider how you can most fully involve students
- read it carefully to see how you can apply it and the Student Book to the provincial, national and regional situation in terms of the strands, sub-strands, processes, elaborations and learning outcomes
- map out your teaching and learning strategies

- start to identify specific projects that your students could undertake based on the learning outcomes (but stay open to student suggested projects that may be developed over time)
- consider how to use the information to develop your own programs and units of work.

Structure

This Teacher Resource Book parallels the Student Book. Each chapter covers one syllabus strand:

1 Environment and Resources

2 Organisation

3 Culture

4 Integrating Projects

The Guide to the Syllabus shows the organisation of the Teacher Resource Book. There is an introduction to each chapter that names the strand and sub strand, with a brief overview to the material that follows.

Within each chapter, the organisation of the text is then based on the learning outcomes. Sometimes outcomes are presented in a separate section. Sometimes the sections are combined. In both cases, the material that follows is divided into main ideas, an example of elaborating the learning outcome, possible assessment tasks and teacher information (this material adds to the main ideas)

Learning Outcomes

The learning outcomes indicate what a student should be able to do after finishing a particular part of the curriculum. In Grade 7, we focus on the nation of Papua New Guinea and the countries in the region. This provides each teacher with a wide range of materials and areas to compare. They can compare different national governments, such as Indonesia and Papua New Guinea; different national cultures, such as Solomon Islands and Papua New Guinea; or they may focus on a particular province, the development of Papua New Guinea or the region.

The Guide to the Syllabus provides an outline of the course. You can use this table to help plan the various units of work. The outcomes are broad and can be achieved in many different contexts depending on available resources and expertise. The Grade 7 syllabus is divided into four strands. Each strand in this syllabus has one sub strand. Each sub strand has a number of learning outcomes. The learning outcomes have been divided into sections. Each section is listed as the focus for that learning outcome.

Guide to the Syllabus

CH	Strand	Sub-strand	Section or Learning Focus	Learning Outcomes
Introduction	Overview of Social Science	Social Science	Overview	Students start to see themselves within the wider region.
1	Environment and Resources	People and environment	The physical and human environment	7.1.1 Students are able to identify and describe human and physical environments of the province, nation and region, and describe the factors and processes that have formed them.
1	Environment and Resources	People and environment	Adapting to the physical environment	7.1.2 Students are ablė to describe how national physical environments influence human settlement patterns in the nation and neighbouring regions.
1	Environment and Resources	People and environment	Changing the physical environment	7.1.3 Students are able to describe the impact of resource use on physical environments and human settlement patterns in provincial, national and neighbouring regions.
1	Environment and Resources	People and environment	Working to sustain the physical environment	7.1.4 Students are able to describe national and regional sustainable practices related to the natural environment and propose possible solutions to problems.
1	Environment and Resources	People and environment	Natural hazards and the environment	7.1.5 Students are able identify and describe the causes and effects hazardous natural events in Papua New Guinea and neighbouring regions and how people respond to them.
2	Organisation	Social and Economic Organisation	Government	7.2.1: Students are able to identify the main features of government for provinces, the nation and the region.
2	Organisation	Social and Economic Organisation	Resources	7.2.2: Students are able to describe provincial, national and regional development.
2	Organisation	Social and Economic Organisation	Overview for action to contribute to development	7.2.3: Students are able to contribute to the social and economic development of the province, nation and neighbouring regions.
3	Culture	Cultural expression		7.3.1: Students are able identify and describe key elements of national cultures.
3	Culture	Cultural expression		7.3.2: Students are able to appraise the main influences that contribute to national cultures.
3	Culture	Cultural expression		7.3.3: Students are able participate in national culture.
4	Integrating Projects	Societies and Communities		7.4.1: Students are able to use the social science process to describe the province and compare ways to improve the life of the province.
4	Integrating Projects	Societies and Communities		7.4.2: Students are able to use the social science process to describe the nation and to propose ways for Papua New Guinea to be more involved in the region
5	Appendices	Glossary		

STRAND 1 Environment and Resources

About this strand

The Environment and Resources strand has one sub-strand: People and Environment. The strand and sub-strand cover a very wide range of topics. You will be able to find supporting material in newspapers and radio programs.

This sub-strand is divided into five sections:

- The physical and human environment
- Adapting to the physical environment
- Changing the physical environment
- Working to sustain the physical environment
- Natural hazards and the environment.

7.1.1 The physical and human environment

Main ideas

This section introduces many concepts. Much of it is based on map use and map study. In outline, the student text covers the material as follows:

- introduction to the physical island of New Guinea
- review of map use and cardinal points
- introduction to the region around New Guinea
- the location of Papua New Guinea's land and sea
- physical geography of the nation through an introduction to climate and vegetation
- Pacific Islands and the Pacific Ocean
- formation of the island of New Guinea
- more details of the physical geography of Papua New Guinea
- introducing political boundaries, a start to the human environment.

This section starts with an overview of the physical environment of the island of New Guinea. Each teacher will have to put the students' individual province into this context. Start with an overview of the physical geography of the island. This is done most easily using maps. Have students study the map in the book and other available maps.

Using maps and the illustrations on page 4 of the Student Book, review the cardinal points (north, south, east, west). This will help students to orient their location in the region. Without the political boundaries, students should grasp that mainland Papua New Guinea is part of one large island.

Use the physical map of the island of New Guinea to study the different environments on the island. Have students compare the east and west of the island of New Guinea.

Some people have said that the eastern part of the island of New Guinea (the location of Papua New Guinea) has the better environments and resources. Discuss with students if this is true. As students compare the different parts of the island, they will find similarities. There are major swamps in both the east and west. Both the far east and far west of the island have limited arable land. Have students compare the different river systems and mountain valleys. Again, the east has more extensive highland valley systems for human settlement.

After looking at the island of New Guinea, the students can then consider the environments within the larger region. The physical environment is divided into two major parts: land and water. The region is one of islands. The seas and oceans are the largest part of the regional environment.

New Guinea and the regions around it all formed through the movement of tectonic plates (see page 14 of the *Student Book*). Papua New Guinea is on the edge of two tectonic plates, one sliding under the other. This process has been on-going for hundreds of millions of years. Most recently it has caused the mountains of New Guinea to rise and created the many volcanoes in the area. The movement of land began about 200 million years ago. The times are so great, it will be difficult for students to grasp that all the land on earth was once together and then slowly the continents drifted apart. (Look at page 13 of the *Student Book*.)

The human environment has come in the blink of an eye in comparison to the very slow geologic processes of tectonic plates. The text introduces humans through the use of political boundaries. This will provide a major area for class discussion. Teachers can ask and discuss with students, "How have the boundaries changed the political and human environments?"

A learning game to help elaborations across the course

Both this first section and those that follow cover very large areas of material. The text will give basic ideas, but students must find more information to expand their knowledge about the province, nation and region. This will be a challenge for every teacher.

Finding information about your province, the nation and the region can be the basis of a game through the whole course. The idea of the game is to stimulate students to collect information. Students then share the information with the class. Everyone can participate in analysing the information. In such discussions the class can follow the social science process approach to the curriculum.

In this game, students play a role to collect information. Students may like to be called detectives, hunter-gathers, fishers, innovators or some other title. The class may decide to play for points or a prize, or for the pleasure of collecting information. It will be important to recognise good information collecting.

In each section, there are numerous areas to search for more information. Students can talk to individuals outside of class, look at newspapers, listen to the radio and seek other sources of information. They are to bring it back to the class and show how it applies to the section being studied.

The teacher may attach some of it to maps. Posting student work may be one type of reward in the game. Giving students special titles is another possible reward. Titles could be based on reaching say ten or twenty interesting items of information that apply to the work. For example, everyone might start as a junior detective or basic fisher. Higher positions could be detective, senior detective, chief detective or fisher, senior fisher, master fisher.

Students may wish to work as groups or alone. Each teacher will need to consider the dynamics of a particular class. You can modify and change the game as you go. Students also may have suggestions on making the game more interesting.

The game should keep students engaged in seeing how what they are learning is constantly being applied in the wider world.

Example of elaborating a learning outcome

Strand: Environment and Resources

Sub-strand: People and Environment

Focus: The Physical and Human Environment

Learning outcome 7.1.1: Students are able to identify and describe human and physical environments of the province, nation and region and describe the factors and processes that have formed them

Social Science is to be timetabled for 180 minutes a week in all Upper Primary Schools. Generally this will allow for a one-hour lesson three times a week. In some instances, depending on scheduling flexibility, there may be scope for a one-hour lesson on one day and a two-hour lesson another day.

There are numerous ways to elaborate the material. At Grade 7, time may be an issue. Elaborations may only be one or two hours given the large amount of material to be covered. In some instances, they may be less than an hour where students have 15 minutes or half an hour to pursue a topic. This is possible where they have sought out further information. Here is an example of a one hour elaboration:

Monday	**Wednesday**
Second half-hour of class Discuss with the class the different types of physical geographies of different countries in the region. Have them divide into groups to each gather information about one different type of physical situation.	*First half-hour of the class* Have the class groups report on their findings. Where are mountains important features? What are the consequences? Where are small islands and atolls important? What information have students been able to gather and evaluate?

Alternative

Monday	**Friday**
As above	Give students extra time and have the presentations at the end of the week.

Key words

physical environment, human environment, New Guinea, cardinal points and map reading, latitude and longitude, climate, vegetation, Pacific Islands, Indonesia, Australia, the Pacific Ocean, creating New Guinea, tectonic plates, islands, political borders

Possible assessment tasks

The following tasks can be done on paper or as an oral report. They can be done for individual or group assessment:

1 Describe the physical environment of New Guinea. How many different environments can they find on this very large island? How do these environments impact on the way of life people have?

2 Using a map provided by your teacher, find the distance between the following places and have them sketch each set of places on a map:

Place	Place	Distance between them in kilometres
Furthest east of PNG	Furthest west of West Papua	
New Caledonia	Fiji	
Hawaiian Islands	Near Port Moresby	
Manus Island	Bougainville	
Tonga	Timor	
Other place appropriate to your province that you can estimate on a map	Appropriate place in the region	

Using the table, discuss the following questions: Which places are the closest? How similar are the places? Does being close make them more or less similar (or something else)? Remember to use the social science process.

3 Draw a regional map that shows which areas have similar physical features and which have different physical features. What explains the differences? Consider terrain, location, climate and vegetation.

4 Look at the physical resources that come from areas different from those where you live (for example, if you live inland, report about the sea). Imagine what the best part of living in this type of environment would be, and report orally or in writing.

5 Compare two different climates in Papua New Guinea. Give reasons for the differences. Explain the advantages and disadvantages of each area (what is good about that type of climate and what is bad about that type of climate).

6 Compare the physical environments of Australia and Indonesia. (This can be done by two groups: one focuses on Indonesia, the other collects information on Australia. Work together to compare the physical environments of these two neighbours of Papua New Guinea.)

7 Collect more information about the Pacific Ocean. Give extra credit for groups of individuals who collect and present information about other seas in the region (for example the Banda Sea in Indonesia or the Arafura Sea between Australia and Timor). Have students explore how important the sea is to climate and vegetation?

8 Write a story about the movement of tectonic plates from 200 million years ago to today.

9 Study the political boundaries of the provinces of Papua New Guinea. Discuss the reasons for the national boundaries and the provincial boundaries. How much do they reflect the physical environment? How much do they reflect human actions?

10 Study the political boundaries of the nations within the region of Papua New Guinea. Discuss the reasons for the international boundaries. How much do they reflect the physical environment? How much do they reflect human actions?

11 Redraw the provincial or regional political boundaries. Explain your reasons for the new maps they create. What type of nations and provinces could be better than the present? Why?

Teacher information

By examining the physical environment at a provincial, national and regional level, students can compare and contrast the information they find. First, students will need to understand the definitions of *provincial*, *national* and *regional* before they can start to make these comparisons.

Provincial: This refers to the events and features of each province within Papua New Guinea. Maps are an important tool for understanding this distinction. Once they have located individual provinces, students will be able to locate information from various media sources on a map of the provinces.

National: The various provinces make up the entire country of Papua New Guinea. Once students understand the relationship between provinces and the country, they can compare and contrast events in different regions of Papua New Guinea. One of the big differences to note is the varied physical environments of Highlands compared to the islands.

Regional: The region in which Papua New Guinea is located can be open to different definitions. This is an excellent topic for discussion with your class. For example, Papua New Guinea is physically part of the region as Australia, as they are on the same tectonic plate, but culturally they have little in common. In comparison, Papua New Guinea shares many aspects of Melanesian culture with many Pacific Islanders. Because there can many definitions of region, you can use this for a number of class activities. For example, have a debate with one group arguing that the region includes Indonesia and Australia and the other that it is only the Pacific Islands.

Physical environment

The physical environment is everything that is not made by humans. It is the natural environment, which includes the physical geography of a place, the climate, the weather, the vegetation, landforms, geology (that is, the structure beneath the land or sea) and the native animals. Students should only be expected to grasp an overview of the physical geography of their province, nation and region.

Landforms are major natural features of the physical environment. Small islands and atolls are types of landforms. Mountains, plains, broken hilly areas, plateaus, valleys and coastlines are all common landforms in New Guinea and among the Pacific Islands. On the Indonesian side of New Guinea there is a tropical glacier. This is a remnant of the last ice age.

A glacier is a mass or large body of ice. It was made during the last ice age by snow falling and accumulating. That is, the snow did not melt. It compacted to form a glacier. A glacier is like a frozen river that moves very slowly. Valleys that are U-shaped have been carved by glaciers. Valleys that are V-shaped have been carved by rivers. The glacier in West Papua is now starting to melt more quickly as a result of global warming.

The largest landforms are continents and oceans. Students in Grade 7 will need to understand that they are on an island. Their nation is an island nation. One of their neighbours, Australia, is a continent. Continents are the main (or largest) land masses on Earth. There are seven continents: Africa, Asia, Antarctica, Australia, Europe, North America and South America. Australia is often referred to as an island continent.

The human environment

The human environment for the province, nation and/or region is everything that humans have created in that place. For Outcome 7.1.1 we only review the human environment briefly as an introduction to Outcome 7.2.2. The introduction is having students look at political boundaries. These are made by humans and have a history. The history of boundaries and colonialism is further studied in later sections. The first work is to get students to think about human-made boundaries. Challenge them to consider the physical geographies of the region and the boundaries that people have put across the features.

New Guinea

New Guinea is the second largest island on Earth. An island is a portion of land surrounded by a body of water. Everyone in Papua New Guinea, Indonesia and the Pacific Islands lives on an island.

Although physically it is one island, New Guinea is divided politically between Indonesia and Papua New Guinea. It is a tropical island with a major mountain chain running east to west across the entire island. There are major swamps in both the east and west. You might challenge students to compare the two halves of the island. There are many similarities both in the physical geography and in human settlement.

Both the east and west of the island of New Guinea have similar natural resources (another part of the physical geography). For example both sides produce tropical timbers, fisheries, gold and petroleum. Teachers might challenge students to compare natural resources being taken from the east and west of the island.

Map reading

Grade 7 map studies focus on three geographic areas. Each one is larger than the last one: the province, the nation of Papua New Guinea and the region in which Papua New Guinea is located. This means that there will be three very different orders of scales for students to understand.

We are starting with maps that show physical features. A review of map reading will be important. Maps at the provincial, national and regional level will be different. All the material on map reading is in the curriculum. You as a teacher will have to determine how much time you have to cover it with students and how much is appropriate for your students.

Remember: maps are a type of picture. The simplest maps are sketches that can be made on the ground, on the blackboard or on paper. Review the following three important features of maps with your students:

- Orientation
- Scale
- Key

The orientation of a map and the cardinal points

The rule or normal practice is to orient a map to the north when it is drawn. When you hold the map, or look at one of the maps in the book, north should be to the top of the page. It may be interesting for the class to orient themselves to the north so that as they look at a provincial or national map, they are also looking to the north. That way they can see how they physically relate to the map. There may be major features that they can actually see such as mountains or the sea. In many instances, they will not be able to see any of the features because the scale of the map will cover such large areas.

The cardinal points are north, south, east and west. We use these points, and others in between, to describe locations on a map. For example, if we use Fiji as a point of reference we can make the following observations on the regional map in relation to the cardinal points:

- The northern part of Australia is to the west.
- Tahiti is to the east.
- New Zealand is to the south.
- Kiribati is to the north.

You can have students repeat this exercise using any place in the province, the nation or the region. Ensure that north is always marked on the provincial, regional or national map that you are using. You should find either the word north and an arrow or the arrow with an N. Once students know where north is, they can determine the other cardinal points (see page 4 of the Student Book). By dividing the basic compass points further, you can create a compass rose featuring north, south, east, west, northeast, northwest, southeast and southwest.

You can have students make a compass rose. Then give them a place, such as Mt Hagen, and have them fill in places from Mt Hagen around the compass rose. For example, Mendi is southwest of Mt Hagen and the Mussau Islands are to the northeast of Mt Hagen, and so forth. You can make the compass rose more complex by adding more divisions to show south-southeast, or north-northwest. Some advanced students may be interested in this. Generally a simple compass rose will serve for general directions.

You may also wish to chose a place on the regional map and name other places for students to locate and give the appropriate direction from the compass rose.

Review of scale

A scale is a type of ratio. Students should have some experience with ratio in math studies. There may be an opportunity for combined work on the concept of ratios with math studies.

The scale on the map is telling you the ratio of how far something is on the map to how far it actually is on the ground. At the provincial level, a scale might be 1:250 000. This means that for each centimetre on the map, there will be 250 000 centimetres on the ground.

A scale of 1 to one hundred million means that for every centimetre on the map, there are one hundred million centimetres on the ground. A hundred million centimetres is the same as one thousand kilometres. So two places on that map that are three centimetres apart are three thousand kilometres apart on the ground.

The table below may help you to understand how scales work in the metric system. Ratios may be difficult for students and you may need to ask the maths teacher to look at similar mathematic units on ratios. Remember that there are 100 centimetres in one metre, 1 000 metres in a kilometre, and 100 000 centimetres in a kilometre.

The column on the right shows you that for each different map scale there are different kilometres actually on the ground. 1 : 100 000 means that one centimetre on the map is 1 kilometre on the ground. 1 : 10 000 000 means that 1 centimetre on the map is 100 kilometres on the ground. You will need this type of scale for national and provincial maps that show areas that are hundreds of kilometres apart.

Scale on map	1 cm on map = x km on ground
1 : 100 000	1
1 : 250 000	2.5
1 : 1 000 000	10
1 : 5 000 000	50
1 : 10 000 000	100
1 : 50 000 000	500
1 : 100 000 000	1000

To calculate the scale on the regional map (inside front cover of the Student Book), measure the black and white key that shows distance. You should find something like this:

on map: cm	Actual: km
3.5	2000
1.75	1000
0.875	500
0.175	100
1	571

When we change the kilometres to centimetres, the scale is about: 1:570 000

Review of keys to maps

The key to a map tells you what features are on it. It may identify physical features, such as types of vegetation, landforms, altitude, seas and oceans, rivers and swamps. It can also give symbols for human features, including political boundaries. The scale of the map will determine how detailed it can show different features. Again this is important for students to understand. A scale of 1:250 000 will allow the map to show many more details than a scale of 1:5 000 000. You can have students explain why this is the case. Use real maps from the book and elsewhere as examples for them to investigate this.

Latitude and longitude

Latitude and longitude are lines, like a grid, on a map. Lines of latitude run parallel to the equator, and do not meet. Lines of longitude run north and south, and, on a globe, meet at the North and South Poles. On a map, lines of longitude appear to run parallel to each other.

Lines of longitude are closer together as they approach the poles, where they meet. They are numbered by degrees. Lines of longitude start with the Prime Meridian. The Prime Meridian runs through Greenwich, England, and it is designated as 0°. Half-way around the world, in the Pacific Ocean, is a line marked as 180º that ends the lines of longitude from east and west.

Lines of latitude stay parallel to each other (and so are sometimes called parallels). They start at the Equator, which is marked as 0°. The lines of latitude then run in parallel to the equator and to each other. Lines of latitude are marked as so many degrees north or south of the Equator.

Papua New Guinea's northern sea border starts at about 2° south of the Equator and extends to about 12° south. Port Moresby is about 147° east of Greenwich and 9° degrees south of the Equator.

Climate

Climate is the pattern of the weather over many years. The island of New Guinea has a tropical climate, as do most of the small island states and territories of the Pacific. Most of Indonesia is similar. Both New Guinea and some of the larger Indonesian islands have more temperate climates in their highlands. Australia has a tropical area; however, generally it has a dry temperate climate with a very dry interior.

Vegetation

Vegetation (all plant life) is a major part of the physical environment. Vegetation differs due to climate and location. The major types of vegetation in New Guinea are mangrove, swamp, grassland, savannah and different types of tropical forest. Forest changes with altitude. At the highest altitudes in New Guinea there is no forest. Alpine grasslands are all that can survive.

New Guinea is very rich in vegetation compared to many smaller countries in the Pacific. The vegetation on small islands and atolls can be very limited. Soil and climate are very important to vegetation. Changes to soil or climate can change vegetation.

Pacific Islands

The Pacific Ocean is home to many islands. Some are very isolated like Nauru. Others are joined in "chains", which are the tops of underwater mountain ranges. Large groups of islands and the water around them are called *archipelagos*. The Bismarck Archipelago is an example.

The range and variety of islands in the Pacific can allow students to choose different islands in the regions around New Guinea to research. It will be easier to find information on some islands compared to others. You can discuss with students why this is so. What does it mean for the people on islands when you have difficulty finding information about them?

Indonesia

The Republic of Indonesia shares a major land border with Papua New Guinea. This divides the island of New Guinea into two parts. Physically, Indonesia is divided into a number of island groups and archipelagos. Like Papua New Guinea, much of Indonesia is located on the Pacific "rim of fire" where there are active volcanoes and frequent earthquakes. To understand the physical nature of Indonesia, have students measure the distances between the different islands. Java is the cultural and political centre of Indonesia. Have students measure the distances to other large islands like Sulawesi, the north of Sumatra, West Papua and West Timor. They may be surprised at how spread out Indonesia is.

Students can make some comparisons about the physical environments of Indonesia. For instance, they might compare Java to New Guinea. Java is smaller than New Guinea, yet Java supports a population of over 140 million people. See if students can discover why this is so. The amount of arable land and very fertile soils from all the volcanic activity on Java are two main reasons.

Australia

(The focus of Grade 7 is only partially on Australia, with more material following in Grade 8.) Australia is the island continent to the south of New Guinea. It is another important neighbour in the region. It has a very different physical environment from that of New Guinea. Much of Australia is very dry. In many places, the vegetation has developed to become dependent on regular fire outbreaks. This means that trees and other plants are stimulated by fire to drop seeds and reproduce.

The Pacific Ocean

More than 70 per cent of the world is covered by oceans. The oceans are the basis for climates in the world. The largest ocean is the Pacific Ocean. It has the deepest parts of any ocean in the world. Much of the ocean floor is still unexplored.

The creation of New Guinea: tectonic plates

The curriculum calls for students to have some understanding of how the island of New Guinea was formed. This is another opportunity for the teacher to show students how scientific ideas have changed. You will need a world map to help students better understand the idea of plate tectonics.

It is only in the last 50 years that scientists have come to believe that the continents of the world are not fixed. A few scientists had pointed out that the east coast of South America seems to fit into the west coast of Africa, suggesting that the continents had moved apart. But they could not find enough proof to support this idea. Then scientists started to understand that the continents do move. Now scientists accept that the continents have been moving, and will continue to move, at between two and five centimetres a year.

All the continents were joined over two hundred million years ago, and they may join up again as part of a cycle of joining and separating. When the continents started breaking apart, they separated into two large land masses, which then broke into smaller parts, called plates. New Guinea, Australia, New Caledonia, New Zealand and Fiji are on the same plate. This plate has pushed against another plate, forming the mountains of New Guinea. Many other forces then shaped the land over time, such as erosion by wind and water, the folding of the Earth's crust, deposition and volcanic activity. (For a review of these, see the *Social Science Grade 6 Teacher Guide*.)

Islands

An island is a portion of land surrounded by a body of water. There are many islands in the Pacific, some of which belong to different countries. Borneo is called Kalimantan by the Indonesians who hold most of that island. Malaysia has states in north Borneo, and there is a small independent nation there also called Brunei. East Timor is half of Timor island. The other half is part of Indonesia. This is similar to the case with New Guinea.

Political borders

Political borders are part of the human environment. They may cut across resources, ethnic groups, land features and other items. Provincial and national boundaries provide students with a good start for study. They reflect political, social and economic forces. They are part of the history of the human environment. The challenge for students is to find out why the borders are where they are. At the provincial level, they should be able to seek out people who can help them with oral histories of how different borders emerged to be the boundaries for today.

7.1.2 How physical environments influence human settlement patterns in the nation and neighbouring regions

7.1.3 The impact of resource use on physical environments and human settlement patterns in provincial, national and neighbouring regions

7.1.4 National and regional sustainable practices related to the natural environment and possible solutions to problems

Main ideas

Sections 7.1.2 to 7.1.4 are interrelated and have overlapping themes. Human settlement is influenced by the physical environment in many ways. The physical environment may limit some types of settlement and some types of activities.

The provincial, national and regional environments all have effects on people. This can be seen by the way people have adapted to their environment. Experiences of the past provide students with good examples. This is clearest where people have adapted poorly or failed to adapt to their environment. In the most dramatic cases, complete failure destroys human settlements.

Adaptations are responses to the effects of the environment on people's lives. How people use resources is part of adaptation. Poor resource use or unsustainable resource use will result in problems. This is directly related to the impact of the environment on people. Other factors that are very important are the population distribution and population density. Again, extreme examples from the past can help students to understand the issues. We look at the Solomon Islands and East Timor as examples of poor resource use in the past. Both have very rapidly growing populations and have had severe problems with violence and unrest. They are good examples to show that poor resource use and poor allocation are not sustainable. Students can then search for examples of good resource use and propose possible solutions to problems with sustaining the natural (or physical) environment.

Note that more information is covered on resources in parts of 7.2. This avoids overlap or duplication with material in 7.1, where the past is used as the example for students to then compare with current information they collect.

Example of elaborating a learning outcome

Strand: Environment and Resources

Sub-strand: People and Environment

Focus: The effects of the physical environments on human settlement patterns in the nation and neighbouring regions

Learning outcomes:

7.1.2: Students are able to identify how physical environments influence human settlement patterns in the nation and neighbouring regions

7.1.3 Students are able to identify the impact of resource use on physical environments and human settlement patterns in provincial, national and neighbouring regions

7.1.4 Students are able to identify national and regional sustainable practices related to the natural environment and propose possible solutions to problems

Monday	**Wednesday**
1 hour of class time	*First half-hour of class*
This work can be done by individuals, in groups or as a class, depending on resources. Have students create a map of their province. Draw the locations of the main physical features on the map. Then do the same for the locations of the main human made features. Then by group or individual, select one type of human impact. (For example, settlements, roads, other transport, communication, power and economic activities.) Analyse how the physical environment has influenced the locations of the human features. For homework, students question people familiar with the province for more information about their particular human environment features and the influence of the physical environment on them.	Groups or individuals report back on their findings. The class discusses and evaluates the findings as a whole. The class decides how important the physical environment has been to the development of the human environment in their province

Alternative elaboration:

Monday	**Friday**
As above	Give students extra time and have the presentations at the end of the week.

In the elaborations for sections 7.1.2 to 7.1.4, you, the teacher, will help students to understand the interconnections between the past and the present.

Exercises begin with a look at the individual situation in the student's province. Each province will have different settlement patterns. Each province will provide a different physical environment. Students can analyse physical features and how they have affected the human environment and settlement. Other possible elaborations or techniques for keeping the class up-to-date are given at the end of this section.

Key words

human settlements, population distribution, population density, settlement patterns including archaeology, resources, sustainable practices

Possible assessment tasks

The following tasks can be done on paper or as an oral report. They can be done for individual or group assessment:

1 Prepare a map to show the different types of transport systems in your province. Then choose one of the following to present to the class:
   - explain how the different transport systems allow access to different resources
   - explain how different resources are needed for the different transport systems
   - explain how different settlement patterns result from different transport systems
   - discuss how the early settlement in the province would have used different modes of transport, and discuss how this might have affected early settlements
   - discuss how the transport systems are related to agriculture. What differences do they make to cash crops and garden crops?

2 Compare the major types of settlements in your province. What are the most important settlements? Which have most of the province's population? How are the settlements changing in the province?

3 Make a diagram of the early settlement of your province. Use the clues given in your Student Book. Where there are no clues, write what you think might have happened.

4 Compare the different first settlements in New Guinea, Australia and the Pacific. Discuss the innovations you think people made to successfully settle these different places. What were the most important resources they had?

5 Collect information for a class discussion on the types of languages spoken in your province. How many are Austronesian? How many are non-Austronesian (also called Papuan languages)?

6 Draw and label a collection of pictures to show how resource use changed with population increases on Easter Island.

7 Find information about the population of your province to present and discuss in class:

- How has the population in your province changed? Look for census information and other sources, such as older people.
- Where has population density increased or decreased in your province? Give reasons for the changes in population.
- Explain how population density and population growth is connected to resources.
- Discuss how people have adapted to the changes in population density. Have the adaptations been good or bad?

8 Have individual students or teams debate topics of interest. Assess students on their ability to collect information, understand it and present it in support of their arguments. (Note: there are no right answers.) Give students a day or two to prepare their cases. After the debate, discuss the issues with the class. Be sure they understand that there is no single right answer and that debates help improve knowledge whichever side you are on.

Some statements to consider for debate are shown below. Ask students to either support or reject the statement chosen for debate.

- When Papua New Guinea has a population of 10 million people it will be twice as strong as when it had five million people.
- The problems in Honiara are about growing populations, and would be the same with or without the different ethnic groups.
- Population and population density can continue to increase indefinitely.
- The most important parts of settlements in New Guinea are traditional (that is pre-European or pre-colonial).
- The first people who came to New Guinea had a harder time starting settlements and adapting to the physical environment than Australian settlers.

Teacher information

Human settlements

There is a long history to human settlement in New Guinea and the Pacific. The text focuses on the role New Guinea has played. Students need to be challenged to study the clues and make their own conclusions about early settlement.

Settlements are based on where people live. Most rural settlement supports agriculture and fisheries in the Pacific. There are many types of village settlements: some are clusters of houses; others are ribbon settlements that run along a road, mountain ridge or coastline;

others are scattered around, close to the places where people tend their crops. Some people will have two houses: one in the village and a smaller field house for tending crops. This is a common practice in Timor, many parts of Indonesia and larger Pacific Islands. Smaller islands are so compact that rural people only need or have space for one house.

Indonesia, East Timor, and the emerging nations of the Pacific are primarily composed of rural settlements. Australia, in contrast, is very highly urbanised, with most Australians living in one of five major cities: Sydney, Brisbane, Melbourne, Perth and Adelaide. You can challenge students to find out why this is so. This can include asking Australians who may pass through your area.

Population distribution

There are nearly 4 billion people in Asia, which represents over 60 per cent of the world's population. Africa has about 13 per cent of the world's population, North America about 8 per cent, South America 6 per cent, and Australia about 0.3 percent. All the Pacific Islands have about 0.2 per cent. The distribution of population reflects the type of resources that are available. This includes natural resources like fertile soils, access to fresh water, minerals, vegetation, topography (the shape of the land) and human resources like cities, manufacturing plants, financial markets and systems of government.

Population density

Review with students that population density is the number of people in a given area, usually measured as persons per square kilometre. To calculate the population density of an area, take the population and divide it by the area. (For example, if an area is 100 square kilometres and the population is 10 000 people, divide 10 000 by 100.) Have students work out the gross population density for different places in the Pacific.

Urban areas are generally the places with the highest population densities in a country. Some rural areas are also densely populated. For example, the island of Java in Indonesia supports over 100 million people, the majority of whom live in rural areas (although the urban population is growing rapidly).

In many places in the Pacific, the population is increasing, which means that the density is increasing. In urban centres, this leads to overcrowding and competition for space; in rural areas, more people means more conflicts over land and other resources.

Settlement patterns

Settlement patterns are an important part of the human environment. These patterns change the natural environment, and have done so for thousands of years. With the students, look at examples of the early settlement of New Guinea and the Pacific. For example, the early settlers to the Pacific appear to have invented agriculture. This very important innovation helped to create more permanent settlements, leading to further developments and innovations.

Parts of New Guinea and Australia have been settled for around 50 000 years. Early settlement in the Solomon Islands is from at least 30 000 years ago. Agriculture has been practised in parts of New Guinea for at least 9000 years. But for some reason, agriculture never spread into mainland Australia. Why might agricultural methods not have been used by the earliest people in Australia?

European contact and colonialism changed many settlement patterns and introduced new patterns, such as the development of urban centres and complex infrastructures. This is a good area for class discussions. Ask students what happened in their province. Have students look at who benefited and what costs there were.

For some Pacific islanders, the results of colonialism were very bad. For others, the outcome was different. Have the class discuss the effects of the blackbirding trade, which took people away from their homes to work as labourers, usually against their will or through deceit. Today, some Papua New Guineans would like to live and work overseas. This type of issues can be discussed by the class.

Today, new technologies in both urban and rural areas are making major changes to settlement patterns in the Pacific and other parts of the region around Papua New Guinea. Mining and cash crop production—at both the small holder and plantation level—are two activities that are changing Pacific settlement patterns in rural areas. Also, cities are growing in all nations in the region, resulting in higher population density and its attendant problems, such as poor housing. Often squatters in cities must settle on land that is unsuitable due to hazards such as flooding and landslides.

Resources

All human settlement patterns reflect resource use, as all humans require resources to survive. Have students look at the situation with early settlement in the Pacific. Challenge students to develop principles about using resources based on the past. They should be able to see where people used resources well and where they failed to use them well.

Sustainable practices

First review the definition of *to sustain* with students. *To sustain means to support or to maintain*. For example, to sustain human life you need food, water, shelter and caring. To sustain natural resources, they too must be cared for: water must be kept free of pollutants, fish populations must not be eradicated by over-fishing, and forests must be replanted and cared for.

Many settlements in the past did not overuse or abuse their resources. But a few dramatic examples, such as Easter Island, show what happens when settlements do not sustain resources. The Easter Island example also shows how climate change can affect resources. Problems come when people are not aware of the changes or if they do not change resource use.

Students can now explore changes to settlements, resources and the environment in their province, for the nation and for the region. Encourage students to find examples of changes to settlements, resources and the environment in the press, radio and from other people.

Remind students that the population of Papua New Guinea has nearly doubled in the past 30 years. This means many more resources are being used. It means there are changes to settlements. It means people are using new technologies. Help students to analyse the information they are bringing in

Other elaborations for Outcomes 1.7.2, 1.7.3 and1.7.4

The following example shows that you can start to cover several sections in one elaboration. In it, you can compare the past and the present in the province, nation or region. The idea is to use recent source material that students gather from newspapers or radio (some will also have access to television).

The following article from the *Post-Courier* is about resources and settlements. Numbers in square brackets have been added throughout the article to indicate possible discussion points for the class to consider. Students should read the article and find up-to-date material to help add to the discussion.

Consider the many discussion points you can have with the class on an article like this. Combine a few articles and follow up the discussions by having your class search for more information. These are good exercises for students to develop the social science process.

State revenue set to increase

[1] PAPUA NEW GUINEA is set to cash in on a massive K1 billion from mining sector revenues as world mineral prices remain high and smelters seek concentrates.

Mining Minister Sam Akoitai said yesterday the country was positioned to reap in another massive payout from [2] Ok Tedi Mining Limited which paid K279 million to the national coffers from last year's massive K1 billion profit.

[3] Mr Akoitai said the revenue from the copper and gold miner to the State for this year is expected to increase by 100 per cent according to briefs that he had been given. This means the State is set to receive K558 million after Ok Tedi Mining Limited declares its profit this time next year.

"The world mineral prices have been very good to the country," Mr Akoitai said. [4] "At the moment the smelters are also looking for concentrate and they are offering lower prices for concentrate from mining companies and this is another big boost to companies operating in the country to benefit from this second factor."

Mr Akoitai said this revenue was only from OTML while other companies such as [5] Lihir Gold Limited and Porgera Joint Venture had not briefed him on their year-to-date operations as yet. He said Ok Tedi Mining Limited had been doing very well so far after posting a massive profit for last year.

[6] Meanwhile, other exploration projects in the mining sector had also showed positive results and some of them would be advanced to pre-feasibility study phases.

Mr Akoitai said a government delegation had met with officials from Chinese Metallurgical and Construction Company and construction phase of this [7] multi-billion kina project would be brought forward to October. He also said the company (MCC) met him in person and assured him [8] that they would not operate on a fly-in, fly-out basis but had accepted the level of commitment shown by the PNG Government and [9] opted to build a satellite town in the country.

"I will be talking to my colleague Minister for Lands so [10] that a land is made available for a satellite town," Mr Akoitai said. [11] "We have to assist the developer build a satellite town in Papua New Guinea."

from Business Section
Post-Courier Weekend Edition, 30 June-1 July 2006

Discussion point examples (related to numbering in new article)

1 What is the mining sector in Papua New Guinea? How are these resources priced? What is a billion kina, how much is it? Is the article current or is it telling you something about the past? (Students may find old articles that are worth discussion.) Who will get the one billion kina from these resources?

2 In what part of Papua New Guinea is Ok Tedi? Who is benefiting from the mine's mineral resources? What kind of settlements are around Ok Tedi? How has it changed Western Province? How has it changed Papua New Guinea?

3 What are the two minerals that Ok Tedi is mining? Where else are these being mined in Papua New Guinea? What does a "hundred per cent increase" mean? What results should people see if there is a hundred per cent increase in revenues to the State?

4 Does this make sense? Is it correct? Is something missing? Do the Chinese want to pay less but prices are going up? What is the big boost if smelters want to pay less? What are smelters? (Have students use a dictionary or encyclopaedia to find out meanings of words and then discuss them.)

5 Where are Lihir and Porgera mines? What do they produce? (Gold.) What more can students find out about these two places and the resources they are taking out?

6 What are the other exploration projects? Can students find out anything about them? What is the Chinese Metallurgical and Construction Company?

7 What are they trying to do? What is the value of the project? What is missing here? Does this reflect any bias in the article? (There is a lot of information that does not appear so it is very hard to know if MCC will proceed.)

8 What does "fly-in, fly-out" mean? What type of settlement pattern results? (Fly-in fly-out is where all the expatriate miners live in barracks and return to another country to be with their families, and friends. Recreation and spare time is spent out of Papua New Guinea so some benefits go to the settlements overseas.)

9 What type of settlement is a satellite town? (It is a town next to the mine.) What benefits would it have?

10 How hard is it to make land available? Who decides what type of settlement this will be? Can we be sure it will benefit the local people?

7.1.5 Natural hazards in Papua New Guinea and neighbouring regions

Main ideas

Natural hazards are a part of life in Papua New Guinea and the regions around the nation. As with the early settlers, people today must learn to live with them. More complex and built up settlements often receive a greater impact from natural hazards if planning is not well done. Students will learn about the many hazards present in the region, and ways in which these hazards can be reduced or people can better prepare for them.

Students will be able to find many examples of natural hazards and people's responses to them in the region. It may be interesting to compare how people in the region coped with natural hazards in the past.

Example of elaborating a learning outcome

Strand: Environment and Resources

Sub-strand: People and Environment

Focus: Natural Hazards in Papua New Guinea and Neighbouring Regions

Learning outcome 7.1.5: Students are able identify and describe the causes and effects of hazardous natural events in Papua New Guinea and neighbouring regions and how people respond to them.

Monday	**Friday**
Last 15 minutes	*Half-hour*
Divide the class into three teams or groups. Assign each group to your province, the nation or another country in the region. Each team searches for information about natural hazards in the places they have been assigned.	Each team gives a 10-minute presentation on what they have found. Remind students to use the social science process. Students should report on the different responses people have to natural hazards. They should also report on how natural hazards are patterned in the province, nation or region.

Alternative elaboration

Adapt to your particular timetable but give students enough time to collect information from the media and from other people who have stories about the province, nation or another country in the region. Another type of elaboration is to analyse articles that students find about natural hazards and how people cope in the province, nation and or region.

The following newspaper articles provide examples of human responses to environmental hazards. Again, numbers in brackets have been inserted in the articles to service as discussion points.

[1] When nature becomes the enemy

IT WAS A NORMAL afternoon in Bapa village, Morobe province. Family members were returning from their daily chores of food-gathering, fetching water and from town. As evening approached, mothers prepared evening meals and children played in the middle of the hamlet, unaware of an impending natural disaster that would change their lives and their landscape forever.

[2] Dark clouds indicated the rains were coming. It began with a slight drizzle and by eight the heavens had opened up sending down torrents of rain. Heavy rains were normal in this area, but the Bapa people were unprepared for the landslide that this deluge brought upon them on the night of January 20. The landslide occurred at 11pm that night, caused by a build up of flood water in the mountain during heavy rain.

Mathias Kau who lost his mother in the landslide tearfully spoke of the disaster that covered the entire Bapa hamlet, and claimed the lives of 13 people. "The afternoon was normal, we saw no signs of danger. We prepared food and got ready to retire for the night. We noticed dark clouds forming in the sky and knew rain was about to fall," Mathias recalled. [3] "We did not know that Pindeng creek located behind our house that we normally used for cooking and drinking would suddenly became our enemy when it brought mud, boulders and debris upon us," Mathias said between sobs.

"I grabbed my torch and rushed out of my house to assess the situation and start moving people to higher ground away from the flooded creek and the mud and boulders," he said.

The landslide struck the hamlet at three intervals, first came the floodwaters, followed by mud and debris which covered the entire hamlet, then huge boulders dislodged by the softened earth came crashing down upon the village. "We managed to group the villagers together on higher grounds and stayed there until day light when we began counting our losses. [4]There were 43 people at Bapa village, 13 lost their lives, we now have 30," he said.

[5] The Morobe provincial disaster office flew into the area on a chartered helicopter to assess the damage and report to the Morobe administration for relief assistance to the villagers traumatized by the landslide. Three policemen from Bulolo walked four hours to get to the affected area from Mumeng station to assess the situation on the ground. They returned the same way. Bulolo MP John Muingnepe sent his condolences to the people and committed K40,000 to hire a bulldozer to clear the landslide at various sections of the road leading to the affected area.

[6] The villagers traumatized by the disaster struggle to come to terms with their loss. In time their homes and gardens will be replaced but the loss of loved ones that perished in the landslide will leave an eternal emptiness in their homes and hearts.

From *The National, Weekender* 30 June 2006

Examples of discussion points to raise with the class

1 What feelings about nature does the headline convey? It appears to be giving nature a negative human characteristic. What does this say about how people regard natural forces?

2 Why were the people unprepared? What needs to be done to prepare people for this type of hazard? How common is flooding and what type of preparation is needed?

3 Here we see the idea again that the creek is the enemy. We are very sad that so many people died but the creek really is not an enemy. Discuss people's responses and how they helped some people survive.

4 What per cent of the people died? How will this impact on the village. Many of the people who died were women and children (this has been edited to make the article shorter). Why would women and children be at greater risk? Do different natural hazards pose more risk for different groups in the population, such as infants, women, the old, the young and so forth?

5 How have people in the province responded? How is this similar or not similar to other natural hazards in the province, nation or region? What difficulties do people have in responding to hazards? Again, how similar are these to other places? What does the location of the settlement have to do with responses from other places?

6 What kind of preparation can help reduce the terrible human suffering from loss of life by natural disasters? What are the economic, social and political parts of preparation?

Killer cough reaches Oro

[1] LATEST REPORTS NOW have whooping cough breaking out in the Northern Province districts bordering Morobe Province. The virus was first reported after it had claimed several lives in East Sepik, and later Madang. [2] Yesterday, Morobe, next inline for an over-land spread, announced through Governor Luther Wenge that it would "seal" its boundaries to prevent the spread of the virus among its people. [3] Late yesterday, the Health Department dispatched thirteen patrol teams to the whooping cough areas in response to the outbreak, this time including areas further south-east of Madang and Morobe in the Northern Province.

[4] The Minister for Health and Bougainville Affairs said his department was shipping antibiotics and vaccines to Oro, East Sepik and Madang to treat patients. The Minister said the drugs would arrive in the provinces by today. He said the outbreak was under control with the antibiotics working better than expected. The Minister said the antibiotics would immediately cure children and also prevent the long-term coughing which was common in whooping cough after other the symptoms disappear. "The outbreak occurs in clusters with no definite patterns or links of spread." [5] There is a worry that the whole country might be affected. Whooping cough mostly affects children under two years old but not serious for older children and adults. He said the disease was spread through coughs and generally kicked in about two weeks after exposure to the germs.

from *Post-Courier Weekend Edition* 30 June – 1 July, 2006

Examples of discussion points to raise with the class

1 Discuss the location of the three provinces. Who and how are people reporting the problem? Will all people who have the problem be reporting it?

2 Where are the Morobe borders and how can they be sealed? How can provinces cooperate to help each other and protect themselves? What type of natural hazards can borders stop? What kind won't they stop?

3 What type of response is this? How important is it to people? What would they do if they did not have this service?

4 What sort of technologies are used? What type of resource is this? Where does it come from? What resources must Papua New Guinea have to get the drugs?

5 What can the nation do to stop this hazard from killing children? (Note that the World Health Organisation (WHO) works with countries in this region to try to vaccinate all children against whooping cough and many other killer diseases.)

Manam volcano gives off vapour

[1] A MINOR ERUPTION was reported on Manam Island in Madang yesterday morning.

Volcano expert Kila Mulina from the Rabaul Observatory, however, said there was no cause for alarm. [2] He said the volcano had remained on stage-two alert but warned displaced islanders to remain at their care centres at Bogia. Acting assistant director of the Rabaul Observatory Herman Patia is on Manam to assess the situation. [3] He would also meet and discuss with the landowners on plans to install monitoring and communication equipment on the island. Volcano observatory equipment previously installed was dismantled following land ownership conflicts but the island's chiefs had resolved their differences and want these services returned.

from *The National* Tuesday March 7, 2006

1 No people have been killed, but the natural hazard has still caused a big problem. What other types of problems can flooding cause without killing people?

2 The alert system is a human response. The care centres are also responses. Who is responsible for these responses? What systems do you need for this type of response system? What other human responses are there to prevent volcanic hazards hurting people? Discuss the value of the different approaches.

3 Here is another type of human response to hazard protection. Melanesian cultural values see compensation as necessary for a warning system even though warnings might save the lives of the landholders themselves. What does this mean in terms of protecting people from hazards? How does this issue affect people?

Key words

natural hazards, earthquake, tsunami, volcanic eruption, tropical storm, cyclones, responding to natural hazards

Possible assessment tasks

The following task can be done on paper or as an oral report. They can be done for individual or group assessment:

1 Research natural hazards in two countries of the region. How are they the same? How are they different? Can you find different responses from people in different countries?

2 Find examples of five natural hazard events in the region that have not killed people. What problems have the events caused? How could they have been avoided or made less hazardous?

3 Each province and nation only has a limited amount of money to spend on natural hazards. Should governments put more money into the prevention of natural hazards or into responses to them?

4 Debates for groups or individuals: Give students a week to collect information and make their arguments for against the following statements.

   – The best defence against tsunamis, cyclones and volcanic eruptions is an early warning system, so government should spend its money on these.

   – Volcanic eruption is the worst natural hazard in our region. (Students may need some prompting: Where are the most people in this region? How many people are at risk?)

Teacher information

Many people in the region face growing risks from natural hazards. As populations increase, they may move to parts of a country that are prone to natural hazards. People are clearing forest, leading to increased risks of flooding and landslips. In many coastal areas, people in the region have removed mangrove forests and reefs which, in the past, gave protection against tidal surges, tsunamis and other marine flooding.

Students will start to find out about natural hazards in the region that come from three main events:

Weather hazards (meteorological events): Examples of weather- events includes floods from rivers and from the sea, cyclones (also called typhoons or hurricanes), hail and frost. Any extreme weather conditions can have an effect on the environment.

Geological processes: These are often the result of tectonic plate movement. This causes potentially catastrophic events as tsunamis, earthquakes and volcanic eruptions.

Large environmental changes: The El Niño/Southern Oscillation affects global climates, including that of Papua New Guinea and Australia. This phenomenon, which appears to be occurring more frequently, results in drought in parts of both these countries. The other growing hazard from climate change is global warming. The release of ever larger amounts of carbon and other particles from industry and slash-and-burn agriculture is warming the atmosphere. This is causing changes to climate in many places. It is melting ice and glaciers, resulting in the rising of sea levels. If the sea levels continue to rise, this hazard will flood all the land of island nations like Tuvalu and Kiribati.

Natural hazards are a major problem for Papua New Guinea and the countries of Asia and the Pacific in the region. Many of these countries are located in hazard belts. The largest belt or zone of natural hazards is the Pacific "rim of fire". This arc stretches from Melanesia north-westward through the Indonesian Islands, the Philippines to Japan. There are other hazard belts or zones for cyclones and tropical storms which also cause tidal surges and flooding.

The Asia Pacific region as a whole is estimated to experience about half of the world's major natural hazard events. The International Decade for Natural Disaster Reduction ran from 1990 to 1999, focussing on reducing the total number of deaths and casualties from the hazards. Much work to protect people from natural hazards remains to be done. As an example of the problems, the tsunami that struck Aceh in Indonesia on 26 December 2004 killed more than 200 000 people in a few days. Most of them were in Indonesia, with other large losses in Thailand and Sri Lanka (which is out of our region, but was still affected by an event centred close to Indonesia).

Papua New Guinea suffers earthquakes, drought, cyclones, fire, floods, frost, landslides, tsunamis, and volcanic eruptions—all of which are natural hazards we have to live with. To the south, Australia is a land of cyclic drought that brings fire and then heavy rains that bring flood. It is believed that there may be more droughts because of global warming (also called climate change).

Earthquakes

About 70 per cent of all recorded earthquakes in the world occur in the larger Asia-Pacific region. Pacific Islands are vulnerable, especially those located near the Pacific Ocean Seismic Zone, where tectonic plates are pushing together.

Some places are much more prone to earthquakes because of the unstable geology of their region. For example, the Philippines are spread across two very active tectonic plates. This nation experiences about five earthquakes a day. Most of people do not even feel the quakes, but the hazard is always there. New Zealand has about 200 earthquakes each year that people can feel.

Students might compare the experiences of the people in the Philippines and New Zealand to the experience of people in Papua New Guinea. How are responses different at the time of large earthquakes? In which countries are buildings constructed to withstand them? What kinds of building codes are in place? Are people in certain countries more likely to survive a major earthquake because of preparedness and responses?

Tsunamis

A tsunami is caused by an undersea earthquake shifting the sea floor and creating the movement of large amounts of water. An earthquake under the water can cause massive damage to coastlines of nations very far away.

The hugely destructive tsunami of 26 December 2004 is an example of a catastrophic tsunami. It was caused by a huge earthquake—measuring 9.3 on the Richter scale—about 240 kilometres from the coast of Aceh, Indonesia. The earthquake was caused by pressure that had built up for about 100 years between two tectonic plates.

The earthquake was the only warning that the people on the coast of Aceh had. The earth shook, but people had no idea that a massive tsunami would result. You might ask students to imagine what it would be like to be trapped in a house collapsed in the earthquake. What could they do to save themselves and others?

The earthquake lasted for several minutes. It pushed water upward by 20 metres from the seafloor. (A boat on top of the spot would only have felt as if a wave raised it by 20 metres.) This represented billions of tons of water. It moved away from the earthquake in all directions like the waves from a rock thrown in a pool. In 30 minutes, a huge wall of water hit the island of Sumatra and the province of Aceh. A wave rose up 20 metres high as the tsunami reached the Aceh shore. The city of Banda Aceh, along with some other towns, was almost totally destroyed. A little later, in southern Thailand, the tsunami came in at a height of 10 metres and it continued to travel to other places in Asia and Africa.

The world responded with many types of help. The people who suffered this tsunami responded in different ways. Some thought it was a punishment from God. Many were confused and depressed. All fled to high ground. Since that time there have been decisions to make. Should people go back to areas that might be destroyed again? Sometimes governments have said "no", but the people have gone anyway. Reconstruction and rebuilding has been a slow process for many.

Volcanic eruptions

Many people in our region have to deal with volcanic hazards. People who live near active volcanoes must cope with various problems that can result from a volcanic event, such earthquakes, tsunamis, volcanic gas, mud and lava flows, volcanic dust and explosive eruptions.

Papua New Guinea, Indonesia, New Zealand, Solomon Islands, Tonga, Vanuatu and the Hawaiian Islands all have active volcanoes. The live volcanoes on the coast of the Papua New Guinea mainland may represent the greatest potential danger to the most people. As with other hazards, a large population in a densely populated area is a severe risk during any natural hazard. North coast volcanoes in Papua New Guinea can have an effect as far away as the Southern Highlands Province. Have students consider what people might do about this risk. What would happen if they did nothing?

Tropical storms and cyclones

Tropical storms and cyclones are major problem for the region. Much of coastal Papua New Guinea is lucky because cyclones are either infrequent or do not strike at all. Storms are more common, often with lightening in both coastal and highland areas of the nation. Other parts of the Pacific are in cyclone areas. Fiji, Tonga, Vanuatu, Solomon Islands, tropical Australia, Tuvalu and Samoa are all examples of neighbours at risk. Small islands are particularly vulnerable.

Responding to natural hazards

The biggest difference in responses to natural hazards is between wealthy countries and poorer countries (or countries where money is not allocated for disaster prevention and relief). Wealthy countries can afford good warning systems, but this does not mean that citizens will always pay attention or that the systems will always work. People in all countries are often slow to recognise the danger and slow to respond with enough help after an event. Papua New Guinea is one of the few developing Pacific Islands to have a National Disaster and Emergency Services Department to direct and co-ordinate hazard related activities.

Many people probably still do not believe that they are at risk. There are also economic reasons why people are at risk: people may not be able to afford land in safer areas, or there may be very little land available. When people buy land, they may not be told about the risk they face. In Queensland, Australia, the government had to make a law against developers building and selling houses in flood plains. Laws are one kind of response. Have students see how many other types of responses they can find.

Organisation

About this strand

The Organisation strand has one sub-strand: Social and Economic Organisation. In Year 7, the focus is on provincial, national and regional aspects of organisation. Students will be expected to use whatever learning resources are available: newspapers, magazines, the Internet, radio or television.

We begin by giving students an overview of government. Each teacher will need to provide information about their own provincial situation. The Student Book provides an overview of national and regional government. Students should start to grasp some of the history of government in the region. Students will begin to learn some of the basics about democracy in action.

Some of the neighbouring governments in our region have been very weak. Solomon Islands and East Timor are examples of the serious problems that can occur when governments fail. Political coups have toppled the emerging democracy in Fiji, resulting in many social and economic problems for Fijians. It is important for students to understand that democracy is important for everyone to have a chance of a good life.

In this strand, we again take up the theme of resources and development at the national and regional level. Resources are a key part for the organisation of society and of the economy. The use of resources is interconnected with all the sections that students have studied in Social Science. This means that elaborations can look for connections with all the material already studied.

We approach this strand looking first at government. Then we move to points about the history of government. Students look at colonial and traditional governments in the Pacific Islands, with brief comparisons to colonial Australia. The strand ends with students investigating changes to government and changes to development or exploitation of resources.

7.2.1 Government

Main ideas

In this strand, students will be examining local, provincial and national government structures. They will also be looking at the governments of other nations and territories in the region.

The history of Papua New Guinea and the region is not complete without an examination of the colonial era, when other countries controlled the land, people and resources of the Pacific. Again, students will be looking at the resources of the Pacific region as a way of understanding the reasons for colonial expansion and the move towards sovereignty.

Finally, students will be asked to examine how control and management of resources is important for sovereignty. By finding out about the resources of their neighbours in the region, students will have a better understanding of the importance of a democratic and independent system.

Organisation

Example of elaborating a learning outcome

Strand: Organisation

Sub-strand: Social and economic organisation

Focus: Government

Learning outcome 7.2.1: *Students are able to identify the main features of government for provinces, the nation and the region*

Issues involving government are always in the press. They may also be topics of community discussion. Certainly many people will have opinions about some parts of government or government actions. All these areas provide the potential for elaborations on the subject material. Elaborations can also be based on bringing guests to the school for students to hear and question. Another elaboration is to have students interview community members outside the school.

Monday	Friday
Last half-hour Spend time with the class discussing the major items in the news that involve government in the nation, province or region. Use a couple of news articles to evaluate with the class. Individually or in groups, students collect more information on the same item, related items or contrasting items. Have the students use the social science process to see how the different parts of government are functioning in the major news items chosen.	*One-half to one hour, depending on time available* Have each group or individual report back to the class about the following: – the information they have discovered – how they have analysed it – what it shows about government functions – any bias they have noticed in the different information sources – how the actions might influence people to vote in a democracy – how it relates to other parts of the social science studies they have done.

Again, simple elaboration can be done using media (like radio, newspapers or television). These examples on the following pages show that you can find many news articles for use on different subjects in social science. You can examine articles with the class and discuss the findings. This should help students stay up to date on topics that are constantly changing. Students should continue using the social science process.

[1] Region a threat to Australia

[2] CANBERRA: [3] TERRORISM will remain a global threat for at least a decade but [4] the biggest immediate problem on Australia's doorstep is the potential failure of South Pacific states, the prime minister's chief intelligence adviser says. The Director General of the Office of National Assessments, who provides direct advice to the Prime Minister, [5] yesterday outlined his assessment of the threats and issues affecting Australia's security over the next 10 to 15 years. The Director-General predicted the fight against terrorism would run for another decade. "Terrorism will stay a destabilising force globally for at least a decade and possibly a generation [and will be] a danger to Australia and allied nationals," he said. [6] Of the challenges in Australia's region, failed states in the South Pacific posed the biggest threat. [7] "The South Pacific is where we can most expect trouble of the kind which generates pressure for Australia to respond directly," The Director General said. [8] "The region's very small states with fast growing populations will struggle to stay viable. [9] China-Taiwan rivalry over ties with island states can further weaken governments. [10] "Transnational crime will keep exploiting porous borders and other vulnerabilities."

from Business Section,
Post-Courier Weekend Edition,
30 June – 1 July, 2006

1 Does this headline show bias? Why or why not? Do you think that the Director General thinks there is a real threat? What other headlines could you write for this article?

2 Where is Canberra? (It is the capital of Australia and the place where the Australian Parliament meets.)

3 What is terrorism? Why is it a global threat? Papua New Guinea is part of the globe, so is terrorism a threat to Papua New Guinea or the region? Discuss what terrorism means to the region and to the governments of the region.

4 What are "failed states"? Why are they a problem for Australia?

5 What is an assessment? (In the simplest form, the students perform assessment when they use the social science process of seeing, understanding and acting. This means that the students are learning to do things that people do for governments every day.)

6 Why are failed states considered the "biggest threat"? Are they more of a threat than nuclear weapons, bird flue or global warming? Again is there a bias in this assessment? What are the biggest threats to Australia? Have the class discuss what they think are the biggest threats to Papua New Guinea. Is there one threat that is great than any other?

7 What does this sentence mean? Where else can Australia respond directly? What type of response is the speaker talking about?

8 The Director General sees growing populations in small nations a serious problem. Do you agree? If it is a threat, what can be done about it?

9 How can China and Taiwan weaken governments in the region? (This is the type of question that students would have to research. In some places information will be limited, in other places it is a fair question if information resources are available.)

10 What is "transnational crime"? Is there evidence of it in Papua New Guinea or other countries in the region? (Much of this type of crime in Papua New Guinea is about drug smuggling. The impact on government is often corruption.)

Pacific nations commit

[1] PAPUA NEW GUINEA has been encouraged by renewed commitment of ministers of the 14 Forum island countries to improve their participation in international trade during the recent Forum Trade Ministers conference held in [2] Nadi, Fiji. [3] Important issues discussed at the forum ministerial meeting include strengthening the position of the Forum Island countries in the World Trade Organisation (WTO); implementation of the Pacific agreement on closer economic relations promotion; improving intellectual property rights; and trade capacity-building in the Forum island countries. Minister for Trade and Industry Paul Tiensten chaired the meeting, reflecting PNG's role as current chair of the Forum.

[4] Currently, of all the 14 island countries, only PNG, Fiji, Solomon Islands and Tonga are members of the World Trade Organisation. Australia and New Zealand are members of the WTO. [5] PNG is a strong proponent of the small economies work program that display a combination and intensity of several characteristics — [6] such as physical isolation, small-size of domestic markets, minimal export diversification — [7] giving rise to vulnerability in the international trading system. The Department of Trade and Industry is currently collaborating with the [8] PNG Embassy in Brussels, Belgium and the Pacific Island Forum office in Geneva, Switzerland, in order to lend support to a number of proposals for [9] special and differential treatment. [10] Topics of high priority interest to PNG at this time include rule on fisheries subsidies .... [11]

The 14 Forum island ministers, meanwhile, endorsed the terms of reference for a joint social and economic impact study and gap analysis of a move towards a comprehensive framework for trade and economic co-operation between Australia, New Zealand and the FICs [14 Forum Island Countries].

from Business Section, *Post-Courier, Weekend Edition*, 30 June – 1 July, 2006

1 What are the Forum island countries and why would their governments work together?

2 Where is Nadi, Fiji? (It is the tourist town on the west coast of Fiji. Suva is the capital on the east coast.)

3 What are the issues these governments are talking about? Why is trade important? What does government have to do with trade?

4 Why do you think so few countries in the region are members of the World Trade Organisation? What does this suggest about the governments and resources of these countries?

5 What does "proponent" mean? (It means "a supporter of the idea or plan".) What other things does the government of Papua New Guinea support? How does this help the citizens of our country?

6 What do these three problems mean for the nations' resources? What do they mean for the different governments?

7 What does "vulnerability" mean? (It means "being at risk".) What other vulnerabilities must governments deal with in the region?

8 What is an embassy? Why do governments have embassies? Who works in embassies? What embassies does Papua New Guinea have?

9 Does Papua New Guinea try to get special treatment? Do you think other Forum members try to do the same?

10 Why would fisheries be a special interest for Papua New Guinea? What other special interests do you think the government would have? Do you think special interests would make it easier or harder for the Pacific Forum members to cooperate and work together?

11 Now review the headline. Do you think the Pacific nations really are committing? Or is this just talk by politicians? Analyse what you think the government of Papua New Guinea might get from this type of meeting. Is it better for governments to have international meetings and talk together or is it a waste of money? Discuss in class.

Key words

government, government service, elected official, public servant, appointed statutory person, traditional government, colonial government, independence

Possible assessment tasks

The first four tasks below can be done on paper or as an oral report. They can be done for individual or group assessment. The fifth task is a role-playing exercise for a small group. The final exercises are debates for individuals or teams. Each debate focuses on a statement, with one side arguing in favour of the statement, and the other side arguing against the statement

1 Describe ways that you can see traditional government at work in the province, nation or region.

2 Create a chart indicating what is good and what bad about colonialism in Papua New Guinea or one of the nations in the region.

3 Find five examples of what government Ministers are doing for Papua New Guinea and explain how this is helping provinces or not helping them.

4 Write a page on the definition of government by looking it up in a dictionary (if one is available), and by asking ten different people what the word “government” means

5 Role-play voting and elected officials. This will require some research of the roles of voters and government officials.

6 Debate: A good monarchy (king or queen) will always be better than a good democracy for government.

7 Debate: A good traditional Big Man will always be better than a good traditional Chief for government.

8 Debate: Colonialism was useful because it showed local people how to make profitable use of their natural resources.

Teacher information

It is important to remember that politics is a major part of government. The teacher will need to be careful in discussing government to avoid political bias. There will always be some bias in discussions. When students collect information, it will nearly all carry some bias. The teacher and students should always look for this. Both teachers and students should recognise their own bias. The idea is to seek balance and examine many opinions. This is where the game of seeking out information can be expanded to seek out the bias and viewpoints of the information providers in the press and on the radio.

It is also important to understand that everyone will have at least some political views that differ as they look at their own and other types of government and past government experiences. The most important idea in the work with students is to build respect for considering political views that are different. Democracy and good governance depends on freedom of speech (that means the right to express different opinions) and the freedom of the press (that means the right to publish different opinions) Respect for these rights is essential in developing good government and can start in the classroom.

Government

Government is the way people are ruled. The rules are both formal and informal. The formal rules for government in Papua New Guinea are in the constitution, the organic laws and all the other laws of the nation, provinces and councils. Other rules are determined by custom and association. Customary or traditional government blends into the introduced systems of some of the Pacific Islands. For example, the chieftain system is formally recognised in Fiji and Samoa, as is the monarchy in Tonga. This can raise tensions because chiefs and democracy can be two very different ways of governing.

Within most democratic governmental systems, there are different levels of government, each of which is responsible for the maintenance of laws and services under its jurisdiction:

Local government or council: All parts of the Pacific, Indonesia and Australia have the equivalent of local councils. These local councils are responsible for local matters, such as refuse collection, local law enforcement, some social services, etc.

Provincial or state government: Both Papua New Guinea and its neighbour are divided into province or state governments. This level is responsible for matters that affect the entire province or state, such as provincial laws and some levels of schooling.

National government: National governments are sovereign (independent) states that make decisions about how it should be run and how its people should live. In constitutional democracies, such as in most Pacific nations, a constitution sets down the rules for government. The idea is that government is based on law and rule from the constitution. In constitutional democracies there are three branches of government: the legislature (the legislators, parliamentarians or senators) to make law, the leadership or executive (the prime minister and cabinet or the president and presidential appointees) to guide the country and the judiciary who judge what is right and wrong according to the constitution. These three branches act to create a balance of power, ensuring that no one branch is superior to another. People vote to elect the executive and the legislators.

There are also international conventions and treaties. Some nations agree to give up some of their sovereignty or independence. They sign treaties to promise to do something or not to do something. For instance, most nations have signed the Geneva Convention that is mainly about how to treat prisoners of war. This is an international agreement. Nations may break treaties or conventions.

Within the Pacific region some very small island governments are territories, colonies, states or provinces of a larger national government. Hawaii is a state (the same as a province in this case) of the United States of America (USA). The USA also has territories in the Pacific, such as Guam various Micronesian Island groups in the Pacific. The French have various External Territories in the Pacific, including New Caledonia, Tahiti and other small islands. New Zealand and Australia have some territorial islands, such as Lord Howe Island and Norfolk Island. There are free associations and special arrangements, such as that between New Zealand and the Cook Islands.

Government services

You can approach this area of study in several ways with students. For example, you can study a list of services or needs that people have and discuss how the government responds. You could also discuss who else (such as churches and non-governmental organisations) responds to these needs in the province, nation and region. The kinds of services to discuss could include health, education and agriculture.

Anther approach is to look at government departments and agencies and ask what service they provide, such as the police, the armed forces, the fisheries department and embassies.

For this kind of research, have students search for information and collect personal experiences from the people in their community.

Elected officials

The heart of democracy is the vote. Voting is a right that is given to citizens in a democracy. In Australia, voting is compulsory, which means that everyone must vote in a national or state election. People are fined if they do not vote or do not register to vote. In Australia, a great majority of people do vote. This is different from many other countries where voting is optional, which means that can choose to vote or not vote. In a democracy, voting is secret, which means that no one should know how a person has voted, unless that person is willing to give that information. This means that people cannot be pressured or threatened in any way to vote the way that someone else wants them to vote.

In a democracy, people use the vote to elect officials. This process can be corrupted if people sell their votes or are forced to vote a particular way. Other problems that can occur with voting in the region include stuffing the ballot boxes. This means that someone adds many more votes all from the same person. In a democracy, the general rule is "one vote for one person". This means that everyone has a say in how their community, their town, their province and their country is run.

Elected officials represent the nation and they represent the people (known as the "constituency") that the elected official represents, even if they did not vote for him. The role of Papua New Guinea Parliamentarians is to bring the needs and concerns of their constituency to be heard and acted upon in Parliament. The role of the leader, the Prime Minister, is to represent the whole nation.

Public servants

A major part of government is administration. Many services by government are provided through public servants. Different government departments and agencies are run by public servants. These people—who are hired, not voted for—work under a public service act. This is similar in all parts of the region. Health and education are two very important services that public servants administer, although public servants provide many other services. Public servants carry public trust because they spend public money. Governments have a problem if public servants are corrupt. The Pubic Service Act has many sections to guard against corruption. A strong government can enforce these sections.

Sometimes government will also give contracts to private businesses to provide citizens with services. These private businesses may or may not have similar restrictions placed on them as public servants have.

Appointed persons

Constitutional democracies seek to balance powers. Sometimes politicians, or the public or public servants will not like limits to be placed on their power. They may wish to act quickly or spend money quickly without following all the rules. They may wish to avoid an investigation into a problem or accident. If they could have all the power, they might make many mistakes.

In Papua New Guinea, the constitution states that some people should be appointed like judges and ombudsmen. In other countries, these appointments are not in the constitution. Rather it comes from statutes from parliament or the executive branch of government. In both the case of constitutional and statutory appointments, the persons or officials are appointed to help balance power and to avoid some mistakes or to correct them. They may be appointed for a fixed term (say of five years). They may be appointed for life. The may be appointed until they reach a certain age (say 70 years old). Some appointed officials are mentioned in constitutions and some come directly from statutes.

The idea of these appointments to government is that these people can make hard decisions without being afraid that they will lose their jobs. Judges are a good example of this kind of appointment. Judges must have independence and cannot be worried about keeping their job if they are going to uphold the law.

Agencies that investigate crime or the results of accidents (like airplane crashes) also need to be independent to do their jobs without fear of losing the job if people do not like the results of investigations. In many places they are statutory appointments.

People who investigate complaints about government administration, such as an ombudsman, are also appointed. This official may be appointed for a four or five year term and it would be very difficult to remove or fire the ombudsman. Papua New Guinea, Solomon Islands, Fiji, Indonesia, Vanuatu, Samoa, Cook Islands, Australia, New Zealand and Tonga all have ombudsmen at the national level. Ombudsmen are written into the Papua New Guinea constitution.

All ombudsmen investigate complaints that any citizen makes against the public service. They and their staff work to see that public servants do not abuse the system. They also work to see that good administration is being done. They give a balanced investigation into problems with administration. Sometimes people's complaints are justified. The ombudsman recommends a solution. Sometimes people's complaints are not justified and the ombudsman shows that the public department did its job correctly.

In Vanuatu and Papua New Guinea the ombudsman is also responsible for a leadership code. In these two countries, the ombudsman can investigate complaints about bad practice and corruption by elected leaders.

The other solution for bad or corrupt leaders and politicians is to vote them out at the next election.

Traditional governments

Traditional forms of government, which have existed in the region for over 50 000 years, are still important. Students might consider what they can still find of these traditional practices by traditional leaders in their province by using the social sciences process of seeing, understanding and acting.

Students may be able to find some information about traditional government practice in other parts of the nation. Articles about the Trobriand Islands or Mekeo people will often include reference to the chieftain systems that traditionally apply in these places. Articles about the Highlands will often mention Big Men, which opens the topic of the most common form of traditional government in Papua New Guinea. Be sure students understand that it is not limited just to the Highlands. They should be able to find other examples around the country.

There is great variation in the region, from Aboriginal tribal councils in Australia, to the Matai chieftain system in Samoa, to a host of different traditional systems across Indonesia. In many of the smaller Pacific Islands, church governments have become as important as national governments in looking after communities. They have replaced or become part of traditional government.

As with present governments, it is important to understand that some traditional governments did well and others did not. This is an interesting area for students to discuss. What clues can they find about the success of traditional governments? How did they treat men and women? Why were women more important in some traditional governments than in others? Be sure that students understand that there are no definite answers to these questions.

Colonial government

Many books have been written about colonial governments in the region, and the class could spend the entire year studying the colonial history and processes. As teacher, you will have to guide students through some of the major issues and basic history of colonialism in the region. The challenge for each class and teacher is to apply the social science process of see, understand and act in order to understand how the colonial past has affected the present situation.

When one country colonises another, it explores the land or region, and gets to know the people there; often a land or region is taken by force. Then the colonial power starts to establish itself; it may or may not succeed. For a colony to succeed there must be an imbalance in power. The coloniser must have more power than the people being colonised.

The history of European colonial government in the region starts with Spanish and Portuguese explorers searching for the spice islands. From about 1500 to 1600, the Portuguese established trading posts in some parts of Asia, including parts of what is now Indonesia and East Timor. The Dutch (people from the Netherlands) followed and fought with the Portuguese. The reason they gave for the fighting was religious (the Portuguese were Catholic and the Dutch were Protestants). However, the real reason for the conflict was to own the trading posts. The Dutch defeated the Portuguese and captured valuable resources. The Dutch then established a colony in Java and continued to expand for over 200 years until they had all of Indonesia and West Papua by the early 1900s (only a hundred years ago).

The English and the French followed into the region. Both already had experience in setting up colonies. Again, these two powers were rivals. They had many battles over resources and trade. This was one reason they took some small Pacific Islands as colonies. They did not want anyone else to colonise them.

Australia started as a colony for convicts from England. France later used the same practice in New Caledonia. The next big group of colonisers were the Americans and Germans. The Americans gained control of the Hawaiian Islands and Spanish possessions in the Pacific. The Germans only became a major European power late in the 1800s, but not much was left to claim in the Pacific. They took part of New Guinea, Samoa and some other small places. They lost all their Pacific possessions in World War I (1914–1918). The other colonisers took them over under international treaties.

As Japan became a world power, it too started taking colonies in the Pacific. Like Germany, it lost them in the next great European and Asian war, World War II (1939–1945). After World War II, many Asian colonies started to fight for independence. Indonesia became independent in 1949. Most Pacific Islanders did not have to fight for independence: the colonial powers agreed to give it to them. This is a good example of democracy in action. The coloniser countries voted in people sympathetic to independence. This reflected what ordinary people wanted for colonies in many places.

Some indigenous people have fought for independence in the Pacific and lost. Sometimes this happened when the colonizers first came and sometimes in happened much later. There are still colonies in the Pacific. The French have colonies and the Americans have some territories like Guam. There are also some people in the US state of Hawaii who believe they should have independence from the United States.

Colonial government introduced democracy in many cases (not all). For some peoples, colonial government was very harsh. Many Indonesians worked almost like slaves for the Dutch. Most colonial governments only educated just enough of the local people to help the colonial administration. Many colonial governments brought in different ethnic groups to do work for them.

Most people in the Pacific were able to keep much of their land. (The Hawaiians are a good example of where people lost their land in the Pacific.) Most colonial government was paternalistic. That means the government acted like a father and treated the locals like children. Many colonisers believed that this was the right way. They held these values very strongly and many of the colonised people accepted this.

Colonial government did distribute benefits. In some cases, providing increased benefits (such as education services, health services, communication systems, transportation systems, development of urban centres and expansion of opportunities for cash income) over time.

Independence

Australia and New Zealand gained a peaceful independence from Britain over a hundred years ago, although some ties have been very slow to change. Australia's Governor General, for example, is still tied to the British monarchy as a representative of the Queen of England, just as many former colonies still have different ties to the coloniser.

More recently, starting with Indonesia between 1947 and 1949, the former colonies in Asia and the Pacific have become independent. All of them have worked to promote development and the better use of their resources to benefit all their citizens. Some have succeeded much better than others.

The most recently independent nation is East Timor, which was colonised for over 400 years by Portugal and then for over 20 years by Indonesia. Very small island states like East Timor and the Solomon Islands have had trouble keeping their independence. All the small states of the Pacific still depend on other governments to assist them in some areas, particularly in times of emergencies from natural hazards to civil conflict.

Each class and teacher will need to assess how independent states are working. Have students evaluate what can be learned from the more stable nations in the region and how that might be applied to failing states.

7.2.2 Economic organisation for development

Main ideas

This section overlaps with the previous section in discussing the colonial past and the present situation. The focus is on resources. You may wish to review the terms renewable, non-renewable and sustainable resource with the class. The three terms will appear many times as they study these issues further.

Government is a major stakeholder in resource use. It may develop some resources itself. Governments set the rules and regulations for resource development, and it allocates money made from the resources. It can use this money wisely for development. If it fails to do so the state may fail. The class should come to understand how resources and the nation affect each other. Poor resource management will hurt a nation very badly. Good resource management can benefit a nation.

Trade is very important for all nations of the region. There are many things that cannot be made in Papua New Guinea. The simplest way to get them is through trade. Good coffee and fine cacao are examples of items that can be traded for computers or reading glasses.

Students should ask themselves where the benefits from trade are going. In many parts of the Pacific, people are trading forestry and fishery rights with very few benefits ever reaching the general populations. This will lead back to questions about how governments and democracies are working in the region. There are problems that can be discussed in a balanced way in class by using the social science process of see, understand and act

Example of elaborating a learning outcome

Strand: Organisation

Sub-strand: Social and Economic Organisation

Focus: Resources

Learning outcome 7.2.2: Students are able to describe provincial, national and regional development

Monday	Friday
Last half-hour Divide the class into three or four groups. Have each group choose one resource that Papua New Guinea exports. Have them research the value of that export. They will need to find a recent table. Have them try to find how much the national government has earned from the export. Then have them judge how government has used that money. What services have been given to people?	*One-half to one hour, depending on time available* Have each group or individual report back to the class about the following: —the information they have discovered —how they have analysed it —how valuable is the resource to the nation and how difficult is it to find out the value (for example, timber they may have to estimate as much goes unreported, similar to some fishery figures) —what has government gained in revenue (that is money for the resource from taxes royalties and charges) —what they think the people have received from the government using the revenues (money) —can they tell what provincial governments have received?

Key words

colonial past, development, resource management and use

Possible assessment tasks

The following tasks can be done on paper or as an oral report. They can be done for individual or group assessment. The final task is a debate, which can be between individuals or groups:

- What are the most important resources of the Pacific Ocean?
- Are the resources of the Pacific Ocean being used wisely?
- Who benefits from the resources of the Pacific Ocean?
- How are the resources of the Pacific Ocean being managed??
- What are the most important resources for the people of Papua New Guinea? Which make the most money? Which help the most people?
- How are people in your province a resource? How is the resource of people being developed in Papua New Guinea?
- What are the most important exports for Papua New Guinea? What are the most important imports to help the nation develop?
- Have students compare development in Papua New Guinea to one of the other countries in the region. Warn them to be careful of bias and prejudice. They might set out a balance sheet of development for both countries. Then write a page on the results or give a report to the class on the results.
- Debate: For the most part, resources have been developed in the Pacific Islands to the benefit of the local population with some rewards for outsiders who have brought new technologies and systems to the Pacific.

Teacher information

Colonial past

Much material on colonisation has been covered. The colonial past saw many resources exploited in the region. In some cases, the original people were left with very little. The imbalance of power was too great for them to keep their resources. Australian Aboriginal peoples lost all their best land and many other traditional maritime and land resources. In Indonesians, the Javanese and others were forced to produce agricultural resources for the Dutch. On Nauru, the island was changed forever through guano mining, although compensation has been paid for the damage.

The most complete destruction of resources has been for the very small communities who lost their homeland totally due to nuclear testing.

In other cases, people have kept control over many of their resources into independence. The colonial past is an experience for most of the societies in the region that is now over. People learned from it and adapted many ideas to use. Some places are still colonies. Some parts of countries are still looking for independence. Different groups are still competing for resources. In some places, people may feel as though they are still in a colonial situation. The teacher will need to guide students to reach a balance in discussing who should benefit from resources and who should find their own resources.

Development

The Grade 6 Student and Teacher Resource Books provide the foundation to concepts about development. In Grade 7, students shift focus from development in the local community to development in their province, nation and surrounding neighbours.

Each teacher and class will look at the situation in their individual province. Review with students how wealth is created and how people make a living in the province. Then students can expand on ideas of wealth creation for the nation and the region. In looking at economic development, again they can consider parts of the economy divided into land, labour, technology and capital. Students can compare countries and how they have adapted to new technologies. These are more and more important to developing economies.

Have students search the newspapers and listen to the radio for information about development. The class may choose particular themes to follow. Give your students some independence in this. They cannot cover everything. Use the material they find to develop the topics in class.

Resource management and use

The ideas of resource use is linked directly to Strand 1: Environment and Resources. It is also closely linked to the work students did in the last year. Review the concepts of renewable and non-renewable resources covered in Grade 6. Review the concepts of sustainable development and sustainable use of resources. See how the concepts apply to your province. Then have students look at Papua New Guinea as a whole.

A good approach is to compare Papua New Guinea with some of its neighbours in the region. Many of the resources are the same, so they are often competing in export markets for agricultural products. Because world markets are constantly changing, so too are the export markets for Pacific products.

Papua New Guinea has tried different approaches to managing resources. The Coffee Board, the Copra Board, and the Cocoa Board all try to increase and protect their export markets. Compare imports and exports with students. The same principles that apply to Papua New Guinea apply to many other emerging Pacific Island nations. Most exports are resources with little processing. Tropical agricultural products are very important to the rural sectors of all these economies.

Copra has been a very important commodity but has lost value over the years. Coffee, cocoa, sugar, fruits and spices have varied in price as exports. Competition in the region and in the world often results in over-production and lower prices.

Minerals—a non-renewable resource—are another important source of income for a few Pacific nations. These resources have led to disputes between government and provinces. The Bougainville copper mine, the Freeport gold mine in West Papua and the nickel mining in New Caledonia are examples of conflict over who should control and benefit from resources.

Good resource management results in a sovereign state having the funds to provide needed services to the population. It also provides employment and opportunity in the private sector where many groups and individuals can help national development.

The business section of local newspapers is a good place to have students look for information on this type. An example of such a news article is shown below.

PNG cocoa favoured

PAPUA NEW GUINEA IS ranked second in the world for producing the finest flavoured cocoa beans among the cocoa producing countries. The executive director of the International Cocoa Organisation is urging relevant authorities to ensure PNG maintains its position. Dr Jan Vingerhoets is currently touring cocoa blocks and plantations in East New Britain, one of the leading cocoa producing provinces in PNG, and will be meeting with various stakeholders – including the Foreign Affairs, Trade and Industry, Agriculture and Livestock and the PNG Cocoa Board. His mission was to inform the government and those involved in the industry that PNG must maintain the current status among world countries producing and exporting cocoa. He said PNG was ranked eight in terms of production among the countries that produced cocoa and number seven in exporting cocoa. He said PNG produced the finest flavoured cocoa behind Ecuador. Dr Vingerhoets said there were two things he wanted the authorities to be aware of. "PNG has the opportunity to continue producing finest flavoured cocoa." He said it was not about quantity but quality and if PNG could maintain the quality of cocoa produced annually, then the country, and especially the farmers, would benefit greatly in terms of their earnings.

from *Post-Courier, Weekend Edition* 30 June – 1 July, 2006

7.2.3 Overview of action to contribute to development

Main ideas

Students can consider different ways to make improvements to sustainable development in the province, nation or region. They can generate ideas for discussion and see if there are any actions they can take themselves. You, as the teacher, can point out to students that there are many ways an individual can help with the development of their country. Some are formal and some are informal. All can benefit the nation.

There are many ways for students to look at development in the province, nation and region. Remind them that there is no one right way or wrong way to develop. What might work for people in Indonesia may not be good for people in Samoa.

Example of elaborating a learning outcome

Strand: Organisation

Sub-strand: Social and Economic Organisation

Focus: Overview for action to contribute to development

Learning Outcome 7.2.3: Students are able to contribute to the social and economic development of the province, state, nation or neighbouring nations

For the Friday class, let the class discuss the experiences each group has had. Review with them gender differences, values and attitudes in acting on their idea. Review the role of government in acting on their idea.

Monday	**Tuesday**	**Friday (one week later, or more if needed)**
Last 10 minutes	*20 minutes*	*One-half hour*
Divide the class into five groups. Explain that each group must make a list of ways to help development in the province, Papua New Guinea or the region. The more ideas that each group has the better. Give the class at least a day for the groups to get together to discuss their different ideas.	Have each group present their three best ideas to the class and turn the list of all ideas into the teacher. Then assign each group to try out one of the ideas. Give them one or two weeks (or more if needed) to see if they can make some contribution to development.	Have each group or individual report to and discuss the following with the class: —the successes and any problems they faced —the impact they think it may have had —how sustainable the work is —what more could be done —the resources they would need to continue work on their idea

Key words

social issues, economic issues, nation building

Possible assessment tasks

The following tasks can be done on paper or as an oral report. They can be done for individual or group assessment:

- Compare a major social activity of provinces or regions. (For example, what is the difference in religious practices between Papua New Guinea and Indonesia?)
- Compare a major economic activity of provinces or nations in the region.
- Compare and contrast two major economic activities in your province: one that is doing well and one that is having problems.
- Explain the difficulties for transportation in your province. What sorts of resources are required? How can you suggest ways to help sustainable transportation?
- Explain the difficulties for communication in your province. What resources are needed to improve it? What resources will people need to access it?
- Collect at least five newspaper articles and/or transcripts of radio programs on any one aspect of economic or social development in the province, nation or region. What are the main points of each? How are the articles similar? How are they different? What conclusions can you make about the topic? Write and present your conclusions to your class.

Teacher information

Social issues (and social development)

Students can look at many social issues in the province or nation and see if there is any way they can help development or to make things better. Simply recognising and stopping their own prejudice against other ethnic groups is one way to start. Social issues cover a very wide range of possible projects. Note that all social issues also have economic features. The following are examples of social issues. Challenge your students to find many more:

Religion and religious practice: Students might investigate different ways that religion and religious practice affects a province, nation or region. They could then work on a specific aspect of religion, such as tolerance for different beliefs. Students could look at ways to improve tolerance, and present this information using posters, songs, letters to the newspaper or other forms of communication.

Sports: Sports offer an area to bring people together. Again they can divide people if they are used as a substitute for aggression and fighting. Students can suggest ways to make sports a strength for the province and nation.

Culture: The South Pacific Arts Festival is a good example of the region working to preserve and maintain pride in traditional cultures. There are many smaller festivals to which students may be able to contribute directly as participants, or to promote by making posters or using other forms of public communication.

Health: The health of the population is essential for social and economic development. Simple health messages can help a province, nation or region. Students could take any health topic (such as malaria, smoking, alcohol abuse or nutrition) and research ways to make improvements. Students can present their information as posters or songs, or in any appropriate format.

Education: Like health, education is vital for both social and economic development. Students can look at how formal and informal education helps development. They may find ways to give more people an opportunity to learn. Students might investigate distance education for people who cannot continue with formal education. They might look at different types of informal education in the province and suggest ways to maintain traditional skills and knowledge.

Economic issues (and economic development)

The "see and understand" approach can allow students to investigate different types of economic development. They may then develop ideas to assist the economy. They may also look at ways of reversing negative economic development.

In many cases students may be limited to writing a report, making a class presentation or creating a poster. Below are some suggestions for topics of interest to study. Students will find hundreds more, both in present circumstances and as economies and opportunities change.

Provincial or national cash: Choose a crop and explore ways to increase returns through better practices. Look at ways for more sustainable production for smallholders. Communicate these ideas to people in the province.

Provincial or national garden crop: Students should focus on women and their production in food gardens. What special problems do women have? How can food gardening be improved to better feed families and to give women more garden crops to take to local markets? Students should investigate the different aspects of the problem from production to selling in provincial markets.

Trade store development at the provincial or national level: Students can look at ways to help people have more success with trade stores. The findings may apply to a province or to the nation. After drawing conclusions, students can produce some form of communication to help trade store owners.

Logging and responsible forestry: Sustainable forestry practices in the region are vital for both social and economic development. Students should investigate an aspect of the economic issues of logging by using the press and listening to the radio for stories about logging in Papua New Guinea. They can include information about other countries in the region if this information can be found.

Computer use for small business: Having access to computers and developing the skills to use them for business is an area some of your students might explore. Students can suggest ways to improve access and knowledge in the province.

Nation building

Across the region, there are many people dedicated to nation building. Nation building involves social, political and economic development, but it is important for students to understand that we separate them to study them. In the real world they are not separated.

The ideal for provinces as well as all the countries in the region is to develop a safe and healthy environment, which requires cooperation. There are national and international groups dedicated to doing this. Government and non-government bodies are working together to support nation building.

In this final section of the Organisation strand, students are looking for ways that they can help nation building. We have discussed economic and social development action. Students may also wish to help development and nation building by encouraging adults to vote wisely. Again, through making posters and songs, they may raise awareness about the importance of developing democracy in Papua New Guinea.

Culture

About this strand

The Culture strand has one sub-strand: Cultural Expression.

Culture and cultural expression is at the heart of every nation. Each culture at the national level touches all the people of the nation. Australian culture, Samoan culture and Papua New Guinean culture each have many different characteristics, and they all have a mix of cultures that form the national culture. The physical borders of a nation are easy to map. Culture and cultural influences are much more difficult to easily map. Cultures are constantly changing and influencing each other.

Some parts of a national culture are easy to see and describe. Australian culture has a very different sense of humour from that of Papua New Guinea, for example. Australian dress is different from Tongan dress. In Tonga, virtually no one wears socks, for example. In many countries the culture of doing business or approaches to education are different. Some national cultures consider education to be very important and teachers must be respected. Other places have cultures that do not give as much respect to education.

Students and teachers are part of the national culture. And they are part of the changes to culture. Students in Year 7 are given the chance to explore national cultures through pictures. The text provides 14 different features of national cultures. This is just a selection, as there are many other features that you can explore. Students can collect other pictures and articles about national culture and different cultural expressions in the region. Remember, cultural expression really includes everything that is visible about a culture.

By examining the pictures in the Student Book, students can see, understand (and evaluate) and act by reporting on what they have seen.

The three learning outcomes for this strand are not presented as separate entities. In fact, the first two learning outcomes are inseparable. Here are some examples of elaborating all three of the learning outcomes together. The elaborations can be applied at any point in this chapter.

7.3.1 Identify and describe key elements of national cultures

7.3.2 Appraise the main influences that contribute to national cultures

7.3.3 Participate in national culture

Main ideas

Students will look at the culture of their province. They will look at the culture of Papua New Guinea. They will have the chance to compare aspects of Papua New Guinea culture with other cultures. The student text provides 12 sets of themes. Each set focuses on one aspect of culture. However, you can combine sets to examine other areas of culture.

Example of elaborating a learning outcome

Strand: Culture

Sub-strand: Cultural Expression

Learning outcomes

7.3.1: Students are able identify and describe the basic features of local culture and cultures

7.3.2: Students are able to appraise the main influences that contribute to national cultures

7.3.3: Students are able participate in national culture

Two possible elaborations are given in the examples below. You may create other elaborations that draw on material in the first two chapters and explore how different cultural expressions are linked to the environment or to protecting or exploiting it. The economic value of cultural expressions can be explored in an elaboration.

Monday	Friday
One-half to one hour	*One-half to one hour, depending on time and groups*
Divide the class into groups. Have each group choose three of the twelve sets of pictures in Chapter 3 in the Student Book. Have them show links between cultural items in the sets of pictures. Have them apply what they see about culture to some part of the text they have already studied (markets or rural economic activities, for example). Ask each group to add pictures from their province, the nation and other places in the region if they can find them.	Have each group present the pictures they have collected. Have them explain how the pictures are related and what aspects of culture they are showing. —Have them explain in their presentations: —What is similar and what is the same in these features of cultures? —What changes can be seen in the cultures? —What do the added pictures and the three sets of pictures tell us about some part of the text in Chapters 1 or 2 (or in both for extra marks). What connections will they expect to see in the future?

Elaborations using newspaper articles

Have students read and evaluate the following articles (or articles similar to these that you have found). Then have them students present their evaluation to the class and explore any opportunity to participate in the cultural expression. The following are the kinds of newspaper articles that students can read, assess and present.

For the first article, a student could draw parallels between his or her own cultural events and that discussed in the article. A comparison could be drawn between the cultures, with differences and similarities noted. This information could be presented to the class with the use of pictures or posters, brochures, tourism information brochures, a written report based on the student's findings, or any similar presentation form.

Baining fire dancers set to woo tourists

THE FIRE DANCERS OF Baining in East New Britain will be the highlight of the week when the cruise ship *Clipper Odyssey* arrives in the province next Wednesday. Rapopo Plantation Resort and Rabaul Adventurer & Historical Tours are organising the event for the tourists. Brian Martin of Rapopo Plantation Resort said a traditional Tolai singsing group and a Tolai whip dance troupe would welcome the tourists. Mr Martin said after the day's tours were over, the visitors will be entertained by the fire dancers in the evening before they depart East New Britain later that night.

Meanwhile, Samson Kakai from Rabaul Adventurer & Historical Tours has called on the people of East New Britain to ensure the tourists are well looked-after during their brief stay in the province. "East New Britain has been a very good stop-over port for some of the world's visiting cruise ships and it is therefore important that everyone works together to maintain this reputation," said Mr Kakai. He said local artists and carvers were encouraged to display their products for sale outside the wharf and at the plantation.

from: *The National*
Tuesday 7 March 2006

The second article could again be used for comparing similar concerns about preserving local heritage and culture. What has been lost? What needs to be kept? How can it be kept? An action plan could be developed to, for instance, fund a library to aid in preservation of vital resources. This could include providing information to others as a way of increasing public awareness and raising funds.

Lost history

By Peter Korugl

HISTORICAL AND RARE RECORDS about Papua New Guinea's diverse traditions and events dating back to the 1930s are disappearing. This is because archives and public libraries have closed or are on the verge of closing due to lack of funds, maintenance and modern equipment. According to reports from the Office of Libraries and Archives, records and materials including books were slowing deteriorating because of poor care.

The National Archives and Public Records Services runs two archives, the main one in Port Moresby and a branch in Lae ...The building housing the archive was built in the 1950s and is deteriorating.

"We need at least K10,000 to do up the whole place and fix the air condition. The humidity and heat are affecting papers. We also need computers to store all our records.

According to the National Library Services, the 26 public libraries built in all provinces and some districts in the early 1960s were all not operating. Provincial governments had failed to adequately fund and maintain libraries, resulting in only 11 libraries operating. Those that have closed are Lorengau, Vanimo, Wewak, Arawa, Bulolo, Popondetta, Samarai, Misima, Daru, Kerema, Kainantu, Mount Hagen, Wabag, Kwikila and Lae. The large volumes or recorded oral tradition are also disappearing as the National Broadcasting Corporation does not have the proper equipment to play the recordings... These records are national assets and they could be lost forever when proper care is not provided. "I am seeking extra funds from the Morobe provincial government to upgrade and refurbish the sound library with Radio Morobe," Henry Tamarua, director of Radio Morobe, said.

from *The National*
Tuesday 23 May 2006

Key words and picture sets

Culture; 1 Rural People ; 2 Schools and religious places; 3 Traditional Cultural Performances in the Pacific ; 4 Raising Children; 5. Traditional artefacts and change; 6 Urban Settlements; 7 Markets; 8 Remnants of War; 9 Rural Economic Activities; 10 Food; 11 Transportation; 12 Settlement and housing

Possible assessment tasks

Note that further assessment tasks appear with each discussion of key words. The following tasks can be done on paper or as an oral report. They can be done for individual or group assessment:

1 Indonesia, Australia and Papua New Guinea all represent three very different cultures. See what information you can find to compare these three national cultures. What do you think their biggest differences are? How do you think they might be the same? (What do they share?

2 Make a list of what you think the five most important cultural expressions are for Papua New Guinea. Explain how you made your list and why you think these five items are the most important. Rank them from one to five. Have one as the most important cultural expression for Papua New Guinea of all.

3 How many cultures can you identify in your province? What differences do they have? How are they similar? What activities bring them all together in the province?

4 Choose any three types of cultural expression and find information on how they have changed in Papua New Guinea. For example, you might choose popular tok pisin songs, popular foods and men's head covers. Which ones change quickly and which ones change slowly? Present your findings to the class.

Teacher information

Culture is a very broad concept in social science. It includes the common ways that people think and act in a society. It includes all the physical objects that the society uses or makes. This is often called the physical culture.

There are cultures inside cultures inside cultures. Parts of Papua New Guinea reflect parts of Melanesian and Polynesian cultures. There is a growing national culture that celebrates Independence Day, Christmas, New Years and for many, Easter.

Papua New Guinea is a grand mix of cultures. It has influences from western culture, from Asian cultures and a large base of Melanesian culture, with Polynesian aspects in a few places and 15% of the languages spoken traditionally.

The picture sets in the Student Book allow students the chance to analyse aspects of culture with very little text. Listen carefully to them to see how much a class can pick out. Then encourage them to follow one of the twelve themes in the book, or to start their own theme. Many may have different interests that can be encouraged.

The pictures show places from around Papua New Guinea and its neighbours. It is not important that students identify the actual places although they may be able to. The adventure for students is to see what they can find about culture in these pictures. You can also use the pictures with elaborations. For example, with the two news articles provided above, you could ask students how these articles relate to the pictures.

You can also have them question the categories and reorganise the pictures to show different themes and aspects of culture. For example, your students might reorganise the pictures into categories such as men's roles, women's roles, colonial impact, rural culture, urban culture, sustainable resources, non-sustainable resources and many more that students can think of themselves. Then they can add their own pictures to collections.

1 Rural People

In countries in the region, most people are rural. In these pictures, students can examine their activities, tools, social groups and clothing. What do these pictures tell us about these rural cultures? What is not shown in the pictures? What do students think the most important missing cultural expressions are? Can they find pictures to add to this collection? Assignments can deal with how rural culture is changing or not changing in the region.

2 Schools and religious places

Around the Pacific, there are many similarities in the region's schools and places of worship. Have students examine the physical design of the buildings. What does this tell us about the importance of these two institutions? Have them look at what the people are wearing. What does this tell us about the culture? What is in the background to give further hints about the cultures? What different cultural influences can students find in these pictures?

3 Traditional cultural performances in the Pacific

Traditional performances use traditional materials. Explore the many different ways that traditional materials can be used. Again, what is not shown in the pictures? What do students think the most important missing cultural expressions are? Can they find pictures to add to this collection? How important are traditional performances in maintaining a national culture? What cultural values are expressed in these performances? Compare Papua New Guinea traditional cultural performances with the other Pacific examples. What do they have in common? What is different? Is everything traditional in the pictures? How old are the traditions?

4 Raising children

Students should be able to relate directly to these pictures. What are the children and adults doing? What opportunities can different ways of raising children provide? How is the raising of children adapted to the environment? What type of education are the children getting in these pictures? What is the connection with these pictures and the school pictures? What pictures would you take or draw or try to find to show your culture?

5 Traditional artefacts and change

This set of pictures can be used for all three learning outcomes. Students can be challenged to make or find examples of traditional or neo-traditional artefacts. They can study changes to traditional artefacts in their province and they can analyse the traditional artefacts of their province. They may be able to collect pictures of other artefacts for display. It is important to have them search out the meaning of the different artefacts and designs.

6 Urban settlements

These pictures show cultural landscapes are very different from the traditional village (which is also changing quickly). What could be done better in these pictures? What are the best parts of urban culture that they show? Do they show any bad parts? How are urban settlements changing cultural expression? How are they helping to shape the national culture of Papua New Guinea?

7 Markets

Which products in these pictures are traditional and which show new influences? Look closely at the different groups, their clothing, their actions and the physical market places. What do these us about the culture? Have students write a story about one of the pictures and the people in it. How is their culture changing? What sort of resources are they depending on? How are they earning money? What will their children be doing in the future?

8 Remnants of war

Conflict, violence and war are still a part of the cultures of the Pacific. What does war and conflict tell us about cultures? What are the cultural expressions that are still visible? Are there any conflicts at present in the Pacific? How does Pacific culture try to resolve conflict? How much conflict is accepted?

9 Rural economic activities

Earning cash is changing the landscapes of Papua New Guinea. How is this happening in rural areas of the Pacific? How are rural activities changing culture and values? How are they changing the roles of men, women and children? Students may be able to collect many other pictures and information to add to these themes.

10 Food

Look at the people in these pictures. Why is food so important? What type of events are they celebrating? Do you think they are proud of their culture? What traditional foods can you see? What other foods are there? How have the new foods influenced culture in the region? What food do you think has made the biggest change to traditional diet and culture?

11 Transportation

How many different ways can you find where transportation is changing cultures? You can use the question in the Student Book to stimulate discussion. Look at the different types of transport. How much Melanesian expression is expressed in the design of the vehicles? Elaborate on this theme by discussing resources. How has transportation changed access to resources? What additional resources has transportation made available? Where has this benefited the local people? Again, ask what is missing in the pictures and encourage students to add to the collection.

12 Settlement and housing

A landscape is the total way the land looks. Looking at mountains in the distance, often you can see no human made features. Looking closer at settlements and housing you will see many changes to the landscape. Some are subtle where the forest is regenerating and some show complete changes as in towns and cities. Both transportation and settlement create cultural landscapes. All settlements now are showing some change to the culture, even if it only a pair of shorts made in Thailand that are hanging out to dry in the village. Examine these pictures and have students identify all the changes. Where have the changes come from? What cultural influences are changing the cultural expressions of houses and settlements in Papua New Guinea?

Other themes to consider

Students can collect their own themes and follow their own interests to explore culture and cultural expression in the Pacific. They may wish to write stories about some of the pictures they collect. A fictional story is another form of cultural expression that you can encourage as students explore and expand their culture.

Integrating Projects

About this strand

The integrating projects strand has one sub-strand: Societies and Communities.

This chapter provides students with an opportunity to do a project. A student may apply any selection of what they have learned to a project. They may study the province, the nation or the surrounding countries. Or they may study some combination of both.

There are two learning outcomes and these are applied jointly in the elaborations. The elaboration is the integrating project. A student should only be required to do one project and that will reflect one of the two learning outcomes. Students can present their projects to the class and that way share the learning outcomes so that everyone is exposed to both outcomes.

7.4.1 Use the social science process to describe the province and compare ways to improve life in the process

7.4.2 Use the social science process to describe the nation and propose ways for Papua New Guinea to be more involved in the region

Main ideas

There are many ways to study the roles of the province, the nation and Papua New Guinea in the region. The Student Book gives five detailed examples of approaches a student might make. The topics are almost infinite. Chapters 1 to 3 cover physical, environmental, government, political, social, economic, historical and cultural themes. There are many other approaches and teachers may wish to give some students the opportunity to use the social science process but produce something very different from the normal report. This is a good initiative for some students. Your task as teacher will be to keep projects simple enough for students to complete in the time available.

You may have some students work in groups if they can trust each other to do a fair share of work. It will be important to monitor the work to see that it gets done. Students can start gathering information early in the course. They may change there minds or narrow the field as they go.

Some students may not wish to do a straight social science project. You could give them the choice of some other type of final product that applies some of what they have learned. For example, they might create a series of posters or a series of linked stories to go with pictures about some aspects covered in the text.

If students truly wish to pursue a project, the more they will learn. Listen to their suggestions. Some boys may wish to compare sports in different nations or between provinces. Encourage them to do this, to collect pictures and to write about the cultural expressions and influences they show. Every student should find something of interest to work on.

Example of elaborating a learning outcome

Strand: Integrating projects

Sub-strand: Societies and Communities

Focus: Different ways to study your community

Learning outcomes

7.4.1: Students are able to use the social science process to describe the province and compare ways to improve the life of the province

7.4.2: Students are able to use the social science process to describe the nation and to propose ways for Papua New Guinea to be more involved in the region

Students may work in groups or individually. The key is to determine what each student is interested in and encourage work in that.

The curriculum allocates three hours a week to Social Science. This means that some portion of the project time will have to be done after class. It may also be possible to combine the project with another curriculum subject. The following schedule can be adapted to your particular timetable.

Monday	Class days for 2 weeks	Friday
One hour	*10 minutes*	*One hour*
Review the social science process. Have students think about what they want to study. What will they see and what will they understand? Then have them consider how they will act. They could report in a number of ways: write a report, present a collection of pictures with explanations, create an artefact, sing songs, and so on. Whatever they do, it should represent the results of their study.	Discuss progress on projects with the different individuals or groups. Have people change or adapt their studies if they are having too many difficulties getting information.	Have a presentation on each integrated project. Give enough time for the class to discuss the results. Then give the presenter continue homework on the integrating project and turn it in for you to grade at the next class period.

Possible assessment tasks

The task for students in this section is to complete an integrating project. Assessment should be ongoing during the entire project. A teacher may decide on criteria for different stages of the project. These will vary depending on the type of project an individual, or a group or the class undertakes. It will be important to coordinate between subjects to ensure that students have enough time to complete all activities. It may be possible to start an integrating project while studying another strand. This will depend of the level of class abilities and the time available. It will depend very much on teacher initiative and class abilities.

Assessment could be based on three steps.

1 The first step, SEE, would evaluate how well the student had gathered information.

2 The second step would evaluate how well the student had analysed the information and come to a conclusion. How well does the student UNDERSTAND and is the conclusion logical?

3 Finally, step three, ACT, would evaluate what the student produces as a final product. This could be a report or some other type of initiative.

Integrating projects should be a fun way to learn about the province, the nation and or the region. See that students have the time and topic that best suits them.

Teacher notes